MW01245957

Dancing
Beyond Covid

Dancing
Beyond Covid

JOURNALS 2023–2024

Full Court Press
Englewood Cliffs, New Jersey

First Edition

Copyright © 2024 by Jim Gold

Published in the United States of America
by Full Court Press, 601 Palisade Avenue,
Englewood Cliffs, NJ 07632
fullcourtpress.com

ISBN 978-1-953728-37-1
Library of Congress Control No. 2024913847

Editing and book design by Barry Sheinkopf

FOR BERNICE

Always

Table of Contents

CHAPTER ONE

Leadership CEO

Tuesday, June 27, 2023
Leadership CEO

I am Committing myself to being a CEO.

This means getting others to do things "for" me.

I'm approaching this responsibility with new energy, love, and fun. I see being a CEO as another type of leadership, leading another kind of tour: leading a larger group of travelers and staff. Moses and the children of Israel are my biblical model. I'm leading my travelers to another kind of Promised Land.

I can play Fernando Sor's "Etude Number 12" like Moses. "Alhambra," too. In this scenario, the thumb becomes Moses, and the other fingers are the travelers. They may tremble and tremolo as he leads them across the desert. Midbar travel is no fun, but though he has problems—dissatisfaction of customers, poor desert food and accommodations on the ground, revolts, even revolutions against him—he must assert his leadership.

Although the finger folk complain, they need him. Without thumb's guidance, they are lost, and the tour will fall apart.

Wednesday, June 28, 2023
What's Real?

What I write seems so real and important when I write it. But once written, it loses power; meaning dribbles away and is quickly forgotten. And I move on.

What is the mystery in this in-the-moment creative realism that, once done, rapidly disappears?

Also, why do I push my efforts to perfect my classical guitar playing? Am I missing something, draining away the life juices?

Could it have its own core of perfection to begin with?

Suppose I made Torah study the centerpiece of my summer study? Would I be protected?

Mostly. Or at least more than wandering through the downward desert.

The very thought of it is scary and mostly embarrassing. What has happened to my once stable brain?

But was it ever stable? Probably not. There were always dark clouds of impending doom hanging over it. I distract myself well with art and business.

Jealousy and Envy

What's the difference between jealousy and envy? How important is it for focus?

Why is the Lord jealous, but not envious?

Jealousy has zeal, protective ownership, and demands exclusive rights at its root.

Envy sees (*videre* is its root) hatred at its root.

What is the punishment for lack of focus, for not worshiping properly? A sinking feeling, downward-trend panic, pain of a lost, purposeless mind.

Secrets

I don't have to tell anyone. I don't have to share it. After all, I always have been, and will remain, a closet choreographer. I hate telling folks I choreographed that dance, or even wrote that book. Maybe keeping my creativity secret is a good thing. Secrets have their own power.

My secret weapon. Yes, maybe better to keep it quiet, in the background: my reserve fuel.

This has always been my way. The solitary, but not lonely, path. Why stop now? Why change?

Thursday, June 29, 2023

What does "vacation" mean? Is work my vacation? Or is vacation my work? Do I even know how to take a vacation?

Friday, June 30, 2023
Learning

I'm hiring folks to push me, teach me, inspire me to learn, work harder, and work differently. I'm really hiring a teacher. What will I and can I learn from them?

As for Tim, I'm hiring him to teach me about Facebook, website design, management, ads, and perhaps more.

Yes, I'm paying others to learn. And that's okay. Even good!

My staff and employees are my teachers.

Learning is peaceful, fun, exciting, creative, positive.

But learning WhatsAp strikes terror in my heart. Evidently, fear and excitement go with learning.

Sunday, July 2, 2023

A crack in the Torah armor. God peeks in, and the light starts to shine. With the advent of midbar power blowing in from the Desert, Torah guitar playing is revealed.

Monday, July 3, 2023

The whole Torah thing is gone, vanished, burnt out, disappeared. *Parsha* reading order has crumbled with it. Six weeks of intensity and commitment down the drain. It just fell suddenly, kerplop.

Indeed, as nausea rolls over my Torah commitment and reading, I realize it's definitely time for a break.

Yesterday guitar came in with a roar.

This morning, Hebrew study, along with Torah reading, went out with a whimper. Totally shocking, the speed of this kerplunk.

Inner freedom has been released but it travels with a touch of panic.

What's next? Learn to dwell in the vacuum. Maybe this is just the nature of the artistic temperament. I have to go my own way, in my own time, at my own pace.

That's the way it is. I am individualistic, artistic, entrepreneurial, a free spirit. Evidently, the nature I was born with.

Perhaps that's why I never join organizations, religious groups, synagogues, and such. But I do take classes from teachers. And I love to study.

All fine for individual, timely pursuits.

Guitar

There was pre-Covid guitar; I played pre-Covid guitar.
Now there is post-Covid guitar; I play post-Covid guitar.
Post-Covid guitar is Torah guitar, playing with God in mind.

Wednesday, July 5, 2023
Dangers of Boredom

Is boredom dangerous?

First comes the vacuum; then, if nothing else comes along, boredom rushes in to fill it.

I feel victorious and sad at an ending, and nervous before the vacuum that ensues.

A day of rest is reasonable, and in conscious control. But beyond a day can be dangerous. Boredom invites darkness and the devil.

Wednesday, July 5, 2023
Body and Soul Are One

Cartesian dualism is an illusion. Body and Soul are one. When the body hurts, the soul hurts. And vice versa.

Torah Guitar is Solar Guitar

Shafts of radiance stick out on all side. The plexus projects good rays while the solar shines in place. Meanwhile, Good Gut sings his own abdominal tune.

Leave abominations in the corner to rot and roll alone until they are sociable.

Solar plexus, along with Torah, run the world.

All together, this celestial gut-wrenching represents the slow moving continent of Abdominal Drift.

But fear not: Abdominal is not abominable. She's traded it in for Formidable and Good.

Torah guitar is solar plexus guitar. Its rhythmic oligarchy thrives in the meritocracy of meter, leaving the abyss behind as it pushes its weather-beaten rhythms to their gut-wrenching belly turning, hot dog-eating, abdominal conclusion.

Gut-wrench play marches in the distance. The good kind. Coming closer. Good-Gut Guitar, gushing in style, waddles to the fore.

Why Publish My Journal?

Why publish my journal?

If I do, readers will get to know how I think, arrive at my conclusions, and live my mental and emotional life.

If knowing me helps you know yourself, then reading my journals is worthwhile.

Saturday, July 8, 2023
Do It For Others

Why publish? Do it for others.

The so-called "they" are not separate from me. Rather there is an unbreakable connection between us.

Remember the connection, and I touch truth and reality.

When I hire people to work, I am, in reality, hiring them motivate me, to remind me that I work for others. Just as they work for me, I work for them.

Even my so-called private endeavors—guitar practice, running, yoga, lifting weights at the gym, language study, the stuff I do "for myself"—are, in reality, done for others, too. Secretly, perhaps even unconsciously, I am practicing for the day when I can and will use these skills to affect others.

Study Hebrew and religion, and search daily for celestial connections, to remind me of that everlasting, unbreakable connection.

Sunday, July 9, 2023
Keep Playing

Time to blend my new CEO self with the ancient inner artist.

I sold Bernice's 1999 Toyota Corolla yesterday. I asked for

$2,900, the highest price, but when my Egyptian-pyramid type bargaining was finished, we ended up agreeing on $1,045. Quite a drop. I was in a rush to sell it on that day, just wanted to get rid of it quickly. And I did.

Nevertheless, I felt somewhat foolish. My buyer got the best of me.

Did he really? Yes and no. By asking too high a price, was I secretly undermining myself? Is undermining myself part of playing the sales-and-bargaining game? Maybe. Why?

One result is the humor of self-destruction. It gives me a good laugh. And I like to laugh at myself. Sure, it hurts to lose, to be embarrassed, have the other guy get the better of me. But it remans a good laugh.

Play means losing and winning. Tears and laughter are all part of the game. What's the difference whether I laugh at myself or the other guy?

Artist in the Closet

I have an organizational and managerial self, and an artistic one.

They work together but also separately.

The first two have been hard at it since June. They are nearly done. The third is creeping around in the closet, getting ready for something. But for what?

Tuesday, July 11, 2023
Moses Moment

Last night at folk dance, I had my Moses moment. Two minutes after the class started, only two people had shown up. My heart sank as I thought, What a bummer this class will be. Why had I bothered putting aside so many aches, pains, doubts, and annoyances just to show up for a vacant group and teach. All that effort gone to waste.

Then, suddenly, the door opened and so many people flooded in, my emotional stage went from zero to ecstasy. Through my mind went the line *Ah, ye of little faith*. Indeed, it was my Moses moment. He didn't make it to the Promised Land just because his faith slipped a few moments. Me, too. No question, lack of belief had dropped me into the hell of zero. And then, suddenly, through the sudden flow-of-people gift, I was redeemed. And it went on to become and be a great night of dancing.

Did wise people discover God or invent Him? Does it even matter? After all, belief in God, or gods, is a good thing. And the bigger the better. Monotheism therefore beats polytheism. One God is an improvement over many.

Belief in a Higher Power smooths the rough edges of life and gives us hope. So on one level, it doesn't really matter where it comes from.

Or does it? In order to believe firmly, you must think what you believe in is true. And the more absolutely you believe it to be true, the better. Can a mere mortal "decide" whether something is absolutely true or not? Unfortunately, there is no one else around but these mortals. So the choice is mine.

Wednesday, July 12, 2023
Return as an Integrated CEO

1. Admire in wahoo fashion my 12 tours.
2. Re-incorporate miracle schedule into my life.
3. Three businesses: Tour business, (local) folk dance business,

book business.

4. Guitar, exercise, and study are foundational, but subtly manifested. Note: "Alhambra" solved by giving up classical guitar career. Which I never had anyway, but always practiced toward achieving. Truth is, I always had a folk song one-man show career, which included a touch of classical guitar. It was never right for me anyway. But it took a lifetime to realize it. Classical guitar replaced my violin playing, which I always loved because it was my relaxation, elevation, and retreat. My in-room monastery chamber of elevation, meditation, and retreat, a place to re-fructify before entering the world.

5. Trading tiny stocks is my relaxation. Mostly under $1.00. Cash only. Satisfies me. I might even learn how to win.

Thursday, July 13, 2023

Just as I am resisting depression through the CEO cure, I am also resisting creation. By giving up my down, am I also giving up my up? Probably.

I need to give up, dump, or absorb the CEO life. And return to artistic suffering. (Not aches and pains, although they may be a part of it.) Artists are depressives. So embrace the depressive life. (Fighting depression is depressing. But embracing it soon results in fun.)

As Barry says, the temptation to self doubt is dangerous.

Evil and the devil work hand in hand to undermine you.

August will be mop-up month. (And it's starting today, July 13.)

Introduction of my living room video studio, for folk dance (and even guitar) videos.

As for new, how about the *Journal of Advanced Babble: The*

Poetry of Something Different. I like it.

August is also the first-ever month of totally free guitar. (Once again notice is starts today on July 13. Is 13 an unlucky number? Or is un-luck a form of luck in reverse?)

Such a pleasant experience was this morning's guitar playing. Quite unprecedented. How would Moses play guitar? Would he use a mosaic of approaches, guitar freedom in midbar style? Wandering across the desert with a babbling Torah Guitar strapped on his back, a desert manna form that feeds the soul. Is Advanced Babble, and its discovery, really a hidden Torah long buried in the desert?

Imagine a *Babble Journal.* Would it free my mind?
Or is my mind free already, and only needs a place to pour it?

Friday, July 14, 2023
CEO Plus

I am completely comfortable with my moderate (not slow, but moderate) "Alhambra." First time ever. Note introduction of the new word: moderate. Will my new moderate guitar playing bring me joy? Could be. I tried a bit of flamenco, and it worked. "Leyenda," "Alard," and Bach, too. This is the new CEO Plus style.

Saturday, July 15, 2023

A wave of self-anger energy building: the rage of a new commitment coming, a new vow, oath, and decision.

Note: my commitment to Torah reading (soul) and running (body) came simultaneously together in the beginning of June. Soul and body. A new orthodoxy rising.

Purpose of stock trading: To teach me to function with no desires or expectations.

To sing again I'll need to connect folk songs and singing to a Higher Power.
Guitar now connects—through Torah Guitar.
Folk songs, and singing—not yet.

Sunday, July 16, 2023
CEO Play

Being a CEO is really about playing with others but on another level. I'd call it "long distance play."

Sure I may be the leader, the prime mover in these exchanges. But without them, they, both of us, there is no game. CEO is just a friendly title, like a second name. Playing together long distance is the CEO experience. But it is still play?

Monday, July 17, 2023
What's the Bigger Picture? Beyond Self-Doubt

Self love is blocked by doubt. Doubt closes off, cuts off connection with the real All-is-One self.

Self-doubt is an illusion, but a very strong one that has haunted me much of my life.

Wednesday, July 19, 2023

Realizing that this may be me, the true me, the right me, means, among other things, that a slow, thoughtful, feeling, a different "Alhambra" and classical guitar style, are my contribution to the philosophy and music-appreciation world.

Thursday, July 20, 2023

Moses played "Alhambra" slowly, thoughtfully, carefully, and filled it with emotion. That's how he developed Torah Guitar.

Then he used the new technique with the power of its celestial connections to lead the children of Israel out of Egyptian bondage and slavery, through their transformational wilderness, and into the Promised Land of freedom.

Guitar playing is private prayer, a solo form of worship.
Folk dancing is public prayer, a community form of worship.

Friday, July 21, 2023

Am I worthy? By even asking, I am answering it with a no. No, I am not worthy. But why not? And does it even matter?

Isn't it better to practice the belief I am worthy? Yes. Do I have the right to do that? And if not, why not?

How strange are all these questions. And yet, they come up. Really, the question is: Am I worthy of playing Torah Guitar? Am I worthy of constantly trying to make a Higher Power connection?

On the other hand, am I at the gateway but fear to enter? What was my sin? Not seizing the divine moment. Dare I do it? Torah Guitar means crossing the Jordan. I hate being a coward. Dive in. Give it a shot.

Dropping the "Maybe" of Self-Doubt

I just entered the Promised Land of "Gavotte en Rondeau" and "Alhambra."

Can I extend my stay?

Saturday, July 22, 2023

I'm reading about Menachem Mendel Schneerson, Chabad, and the Lubavitcher movement. Look at all he accomplished.

I'm jealous. A jealous wind is crushing my bones this morning, destroying any possibility of joy, growth. Or expansion. It feels awful; I hate myself for having it. But I do.

Can anything good come out of jealousy? Can I reinterpret it so I can find something positive and then *like* my jealousy, and myself along with it?

Jealousy breeds competition. It also feeds it. Although, to me, competition feels terrible, it can be a motivator.

I know I am right. Why hide any longer? Okay, I won't. Time to change my reaction. Learn and practice loving my competition. Thank them for inspiring me to work harder to achieve what they have achieved. That is the healthy, positive way of looking at jealousy and competition.

So Schneerson's achievements and genius will now inspire me to work and study harder. Good!

Monday, July 24, 2023

Guitar: Rabbit and bull.
Bunny (rabbit) guitar: light, fast, soft, but not weak
Bull guitar: loud, heavy, strong, and slow.
The two warm-up styles are good, but different.
The Bull of Heaven focuses on index and fingers.
Rabbit, the same.
Bull and rabbit have to meet in the middle and form a synthesis, a combo, the synthesis/synthetic animal, a rabbobull or bullorabbit. This new animal is a step beyond the fuck-it-all-and-let-it rip combo.

It is an abdominal, phenomenal, solar plexus focused, rhythm and meter, feel the beat animal. Twins meet when the feel the beat. Rabbobull marries Meter. Bullorabbit marries Rhythm. All four of them become dancers.

Rhythm and Meter smile happily. They know they belong to a grand music family dancing on the same dance floor.

Rabbobull and his sister, Bullorabbit, dance together. So do Rhythm and Meter. Changing partners back and forth, they glide in square or folk dance steps across the shining dance floor.

Tuesday, July 25, 2023

Jump in. Go with sloppy until it relaxes, feels comfortable, focused, and gets better "by itself."

Synthetic Sloppy is cold and stiff. But once warmed up, it (she, he, it, they) flies like the wind.

Dive In: The Next Stage

Dive in is the next stage. August is its practice month. Sloppy, imperfect doesn't matter. The important thing is to dive in. Then things start to happen.

Why is it the next stage? What else is left? There's nothing to startle or stop me. I've done everything else, tried it all. There's nothing left—no impediments, blocks, nothing.

Wednesday, July 26, 2023
The Hasidic Folk Dance Domain

I can't believe how brilliant the writings of Chabad are. How come I never knew this? Maybe I'm just ready for it. Is this the secret Hasid displaying itself, coming out of my body and mind at this advanced age? Was that the cause of my secret attraction to the black-coated and -dressed Hassidim? Their passion and visual off-the-wall clothing, attitude, and craziness—divine madness, really—has always fascinated and attracted me. It feels like the time is ripe, and all this attraction is now coming home to roost. Opening a new direction. Actually, revealing an old but partially hidden one.

I am already a closet Hasid in my worship of passion, which no doubt means the Higher Power in disguise. Will I now become and display my outward Hasid? I'm ready, willing, able, and happy to do so. And I already have the venue where I weekly do it: folk dancing.

Folk dancing is my rabbinate, my secret Hasidic domain. And not so secret at that. It is a short step to seeing it that way, and admitting, or rather, realizing it.

Since I'm not a joiner, I doubt I will ever join Chabad. On the other hand, maybe I already have. Only it is called "folk dancing."

Chabad expresses intellectually what folk dancing does to me, and us, emotionally. The music and dance and community all moving together create the magic sparks that light the fire of union. I like Chabad because it is meant for all; it is universal (meant not only for Jews). Just like folk dancing.

Guitar:

Dive into scales right away. (No "warm-up" in the old "traditional" sense.) Grab meter and rhythm immediately.

(Even add speed.)

Use abs and abdomen. (Note how my stomach is churning already!)

Introducing Dive-In Guitar

Dive into passion through meter and rhythm.

Torah study loves intellect, and the majesty of learning while diving-in, through meter and rhythm, feeds and ex-presses emotion.

Dive-In Guitar brings out the passion side of Torah Guitar.

Thursday, July 27, 2023

Video dances in living room. Dive in right away: Guitar scales adding rhythm, meter, and a beat.

Chabad: Find the good concealed in the *tzuras*.

Friday, July 28, 2023

Lots of anger words in D'varim this morning, but for today I see them as "energy" words.

Less knee pain today. Is it due to rest, to the coalescing of pain-and-suffering idea. I want and hope for the latter. Since I do, make it so. Consider "pain and suffering" for my limbs. And create a new "goal"—to understand the deeper significance of the pain and suffering in my knee. Pain forces you to pay attention. From there, I move up to suffering, which speaks of pain's cosmic condition and purpose. It asks: What is the greater purpose (suffering) of my knee and its pain? Purposeless pain is affliction.

Purposeful pain creates a window into significance, meaning. And thus lessens the pain!

Guitar: Going well.

Thumb 90–95 percent for one week. See where it leads.

Al and Ley. Alley.

Sunday, July 30, 2023

I established three-month goals in June, namely Torah reading daily and running. Both have been reached, achieved, and are on their way.

Now, today, I have a weekly goal: to do well on my upcoming stress test. I'm practicing on the treadmill. I now have an all-exercise goal until next Thursday.

Establish weekly goals? Something to consider.

"The Perfect Is The Enemy Of The Good"

Guitar idea:

I will never get "Alhambra" or "Leyenda" right. And that's okay. "The perfect is the enemy of the good."

An excellent idea and motto and idea for my next phase. Looking at things in this "realistic" way, my "Alhambra" is good, so is my "Leyenda," and my classical guitar playing, and my website design, and my writing, and many other things I do. The only problem for me was and is that they are not *perfect*. And have rarely been so. This imperfection has plagued me mucho. Especially in classical guitar.

Indeed, I have ever strived for perfection. Of course, it is rarely achieved.

But with the idea that "the perfect is the enemy of the good," my next phase will be to move past, even drop, my goals of perfection, and instead, accept the good, my good, and, on all levels, dive into it. This is a major achievement, perfect in its imperfection!

I'll start thinking like this today.

First, regarding Cathie, Tim, and my website design: Why not have them both? Sure it's a bit messy and uncomfortable. But that is the perfect definition of imperfection.

But instead of perfect, it will be good.

As for guitar, saying goodbye to the perfect roads of "Alhambra," "Leyenda," and all my playing, and saying hello to my good player self, brings a reign of inner peace.

As for my website, as an amateur designer, I'm okay, and even good enough. As such, I can even "compete" with the professionals.

Monday, July 31, 2023
Voice and Social Activism

Exercise. The week program. Run it with weekly goals for three months, August 1–November 1.

This week: gym:, running (treadmill), yoga, weights.

Hebrew and guitar: Bounce them along, on their way, carry their habit burden lightly.

Hebrew (Torah)

Read it, hear it, speak it. Read, hear, speak.

By listening to the Hebrew Torah reading, I'm missing an emotional commitment. Add speaking, and I've got a complete commitment. (Influenced by Zach and his Turkish commitment.)

Add this to extras burdens of voice and neighborhood activism. Anything good here? Meet my neighbors, work together, be social, and that's fun, relaxing, a good "break." Yet I feel the tyranny of perfection and fulfillment creeping up, reaching in to grab my mind and soul. My shoulders feel the burden; an incipient slight headache clouds the sky.

This is a call to get involved politically (voice and Hebrew) on a local level, something I have never done before. Like Hebrew language and religion, nice to stand on the side and watch—but to jump in, dive in, be part of it, a voice. . .and make it part of my fun through fulfillment vision?

Tuesday, August 1, 2023

How to monetize my YouTube channel, reach 1,000 subscribers, organize and promote the channel?

Guitar: Mama and Papa thumb want to promote and proudly show off their three (Miki, Jimmy, and Jonny) fingers.

We're a family!

Wednesday, August 2, 2023

Best a.m. ever. Woke up at 4:30 a.m. Hebrew, then light exercise. Guitar, then light exercise. Journal, (and a touch of email). Then full exercise.

Guitar: Happy Fingers!

So-called sleepiness is my wall of resistance to climb the ladder. Faster fingers wake them up. Speed lifts the soul from the ground and creates flight.

Flying power smooth and softly flows through the fingers.

Glory, mad, and wild digits ascend, passing though the fluffy clouds, and into the clear blue shining of digital hand union.

Thursday, August 3, 2023

Zach left. New 6-week goal until he and David return.

1. Exercise: Daily to gym.

2. YouTube channel: In CEO mode and style: Hire someone to organize and build up my Jim Gold YouTube channel. Does such a person exist? We'll see. Its CEO thinking on the nest level.

Torah translations: It's disillusioning to realize that the experts, although knowledgeable, also interpret and create their translations. The fact that they do, though, gives me the power to do it to, use what knowledge I have to interpret and create my own Torah translations.

CEO: Next Step

I just got a chill. Seems my direction as a CEO has solidified. I looked up YouTube development on Google and found so many YouTube developers. They are all looking for work!

CEO, leadership, social directing, the next step.

I don't have patience for the details; I'm into the bigger picture.

Friday, August 4, 2023
Living Room

I need a place to let loose on the guitar—and probably everything else. What better place than my living room, a place to live, and it has room.

Letting loose starts with guitar, but doesn't end there.

Saturday, August 5, 2023

Pure art. Let loose. Make it personal. Between H. and me. The audience is part of H. I reach the audience through H. Focus on and meet with H., and the audience comes along free, comes along for the ride.

Sunday, August 6, 2023

Feeling a bit overwhelmed by my tour focus, and somewhat squashed and down. I'm being squeezed into an all-tour corner, and losing (giving up) my artistic connections. Business and tours are overwhelming my arts. I don't want to go backward and waste unhappy time in the passing cloud. I've been there. I know clouds exist, float above me, block out the sun, then pass. It is my choice to embrace or ignore them. I now choose to ignore them by doing my duty, namely committing to sunny things, focusing on doing miracle schedule processes until they pass.

Speaking is the next step. I don't know why, but I know it's right. The Davidic inspiration.

Life Blood and Hobby

Back to arts as my life blood, and tours, business, and money as my hobby.

Monday, August 7, 2023
The Beauty of Languages

What do I like about languages?

I like the sound of the word, its sight and shape on the page, and its taste and feel in my mouth. That adds up to four senses. No sense of smell involved yet, although eventually, if I think about it, I may add it.

How does a word smell? Imagine sniffing at a vowel, smelling a consonant. That's why there is no reason to read fast, to rush through, run past, and thus bypass the beauty of a language.

I read very slowly, and when I come upon a new word, I relish it, dive into it, and research it like hell. In that sense, I love the fires. They heat up my brain and, in the process, drive my mind from the diabolical furnace below up and through the pearly gates, straight into heaven.

סור is my Hebrew word of the day. She is now personal, part of my family. See H.'s personal involvement in my life today through this word. In doing so, I'll also want to meet the relatives in my new word's family by studying them through the *Etymological Dictionary of Biblical Hebrew* by Matityahu Clark, based on the commentaries of Samson Raphael Hirsch.

Politics

To be or not to be. Trump or non-Trump. Politics is a form of war. It's not about truth, but about winning. Thus so-called "facts" used in political arguments are really only verbal weapons aimed at the enemy in order to convince and beat them, and win the battle.

For truth, you need to be above the fray, and be impartial.

Gold Nuggets, The World of Jim Gold International: Possible subtitles: Blogovsko Horo. Jim Thinking Stuff. Mining in the Age of Folk Dance. Creative Veins, Vains, and More.

Introducing the Living Room Video Studio

Gold Nuggets would be a personal cogitation, meditation, stray thoughts, dreams and visions "newsletter" about the travels of my mind. In blog form. Subjects: Fiction, stories, dances, tours, guitar, readings, all and any. Add stories about folk dancing and travel in each country and tour. 13 blogs, 13 countries. Bi-weekly issues. (Weekly: too much, monthly: too little.)

Morning thoughts after a good night's sleep: Will I ever put an effort into creating Gold Nuggets? I need a reason, a purpose. And it has to be fun. Can I, should I, make it fun? Yes. The final question is: How?

Guitar Victory

I went all the way back to square one, played it as slowly as possible, saw no progress from forty years ago to today. . .and here's the victory: I didn't feel defeated, inferior, or even bad. In fact, I felt calm and partly good. I accepted Mr. Slow as part of my family. No problem.

It's a new kind of "good feeling." Partly due to my new CEO self-definition. I am no longer defining myself as a guitarist, so all the self-pressure is off. I am free to go whatever way I want. All directions are open, whether slow, fast, both, or direction-or-speed still unknown. I'm out of the desert wilderness, taking my first steps into the Promised Land. Where will this lead? What will happen? We'll see. But my first guitar steps bring a good Red Castle ("Alhambra") feeling.

The New Promised Land Audience

Playing guitar in my Personal Living Room Video Studio is re revealing new aspects of my post-Covid, pre-CEO thinking, perhaps even revealing a new level of my upcoming Gold Nugget mind. As I play "Alhambra," I see every note, and especially the notes produced by my index finger, going straight into the hearts and minds of the new audience. All notes are expressing the new and free me. I play whatever way I want, whichever way I feel. My new audience, seeing and hearing me play in my Personal

Living Room Video Studio, is now part of my living room family.

On one level, it no longer matters to me what they think. But better and truly, there has been a qualitative change: I've arrived at a new level. Quantities of Covid pain, pounding on my pre-Covid mind, transformed it by creating a qualitative leap, a thorough change. Plato, Marx, and Hegel's dialectics were right. This "new" audience is now part of my family. And it really doesn't matter how I think. They love and accept all of me, with love, kindness, and even happiness. My ancient, desert, wilderness audience, filled with its barbs, unkind thoughts, and subtly wishing for my destruction, are gone. My audience has become my fan club, openly rooting for me.

Out of the wilderness, into living-room-video-studio glory: This new family has metamorphosed into my Promised Land audience.

Tuesday, August 8, 2023

The idea is to live in two worlds: the crazy world of heaven, and the stress-filled world of earth.

And accept both.

The root of "gratitude" is *gratis*.
Gratitude is free.
Happiness is free because it is a thought.

How can I introduce crazy fiction into my life? Crazy fiction is so relaxing and freeing; it puts me in touch with the higher world of Crazy Heaven.

Healthy and good for me, and for others, where can I find the mad celestials?

If happiness is a thought, then bring them to me.

Already the crazy plural in the singular.

CHAPTER TWO

Gold Nugget
Leadership Life

Wednesday, August 9, 2023
What Is the Gold Nugget (Folk Dance) Life?

Let's start with posture: As a start, the Gold Nugget Life (GNL) means standing straight and tall.

What about fiction? And fictions? Should I make a separate journal and folder for New Leaf Fiction, and another for Gold Nugget Leadership? Should I separate fiction from so-called reality? Or should they be combined? Since All-is-One, why not express, expose, and demonstrate this truth by creating one All-is-One journal? And put it all in one folder? Sounds daring. I like to dare. But, although on a higher, refined vibrational level, fiction and reality are the same, does that make it right?

Is the Gold Nugget Life a higher-level life? Yes. Then keeping the scattered, flying, myriad parts of the wandering, jungle-monkey mind together in one journal, is correct. Being correct makes it right.

New Audience and Technology

What's new in Gold Nugget Guitar Life? No more in-person audiences to criticize and taunt me. The video camera is my new audience. As shield and protector, it is forgiving, and filters out fears. Yes, video camera is my new audience. For folk dancing, too.

Friday, August 11, 2023
A Wow Through and Qualitative Leap

Stuff is flowing in tour-wise. Our Greek tour is filling seemingly "by itself." An astounding, astonishing development: Maybe I don't have to hire a social media expert—although I still will; maybe I don't have to work so hard on getting more customers to fill my tours. Maybe I have enough. And I can relax, and do other things. Maybe I'm on the right path, can wait around, be patient, and simply keep doing what I'm doing.

Meeting Amalek

Part of the Gold Nugget life is dumping Amalek. I met him yesterday. Underneath his wide black night hat, he had his usual sneer. (No daylight for him.)

What a downer! All he said was "So what?" How depressing. No reasoning with him. In fact, Amalek is depression. And a danger to the Teaneck community, and my personal sanity.

In the future, I will deal with his visitations by burning his ugly hide, and throwing his remains out the window. As a perfect example of a perishable, Amalek must be eliminated. The garbage can is his true home.

The bible—Torah and New Testament—is a personal guide to freedom. Read it as such.

Saturday, August 12, 2023

Something breaks and goes wrong every day. Today it's my website. The daily question is: How to stay on the path, and fix it?

Creativity Revisited

As I read about problems in my website, a fleeting familiar feeling of sadness and desperation crept into my Saturday morning brain. Part of me loves this black cloud. It reminds me of my old depression-as-prelude-to-creation motivation mode.

And I like to create. But do I need the sad rain of a downer cloud to do it? Go with it, milk its contents, write as I embrace it? Or give it up? Or let it pass?

Sunday, August 13, 2023
The Happy Guitarist: Practice is the Grand Reminder—
Quadruple Your Pleasure in the Land of Happy Thighs

During last night's yoga practice, I had my first good thigh feeling. Can I stand such goodness? And remain, at least for a few moments, in the Promised Land?

To stand under the sun of success and live in the happy moment: That's the new challenge. A good guitarist begins the day with a Happy Pavane. Joining the happy souls dancing in Elysian fields, he enters the land of the dead where they really live!

A happy guitarist wants to be in both. He *is* in both. How to make periodic visits? Practice is the grand reminder. Remember to practice.

Monday, August 14, 2023
Coding and Web Design

I can't believe I am saying this, but I am: Becoming and being a CEO is boring. Maybe I've just gone as far as I can, want, or need to go. Filling my tours and collecting money from my customers is fun, up to a point. But after awhile, even that becomes boring. I'm just repeating myself, spinning my wheels, filling my time with rote and boring tasks.

Where is the excitement, romance and adventure? I need stuff that wakes me up, makes stand up and dance!

Yes, CEO-wise, I've gone as far as I need to go. Time to add on, move on to something else, creative, artistic and adventurous. But to what? Coding?

And what happened to all my plans for making folk dance videos, guitar videos, readings, books sales? Have all their energies drifted away? Have they *too* gone as far as they can go?

Are they all becoming simply more of the same, rote work that has become so "easy" it is boring—no challenge, excitement, romance, adventure, or energy left in them?

I hope not. But hoping does not make it so.

Perhaps they too *have* gone as far as I can, want, or need them to go. Giving up these old loves, along with writing fiction (my journal is so natural, it's part of me) is rather sad. But it could be true.

Fame and fortune have dribbled away as motivations. Perhaps the love of excitement, romance, and adventure were always the catalysts that really drove me on. Achieving fame and fortune were part of that romance and adventure.

How, if ever, to re-invigorate them? New goals and purposes would do it. At the moment, I have none.

Artistic Adventures

I've steadied the ship. After sailing into necessary and needed organizational and management CEO side trip waters, with its discovery of new lands, it's now back to the artistic life. Is being a CEO an art? Can one be an artistic CEO? Maybe.

I've come home again: How to add CEO to my artistic repertoire? How to make my JGI tour company part of my artistic adventure.

I need and needed artistic technical help. That's what hiring a social (digital) media marketer, with his web designer, was and is all about.

Perhaps the art of CEO is how to design a company along with its people. Or maybe "CEO" is the wrong title for me. It so smacks of boardrooms, group decisions, and even bureaucracy. "Leader," "entrepreneur," even "artist," is better. After all, even Pablo Picasso had help.

CEO Art

The CEO art is to design a tapestry out of people. I still don't like the CEO term, but this artistic definition is better. So I'll keep the term but redefine it. This way, it joins "leader," "entrepreneur," and "artist."

Tuesday, August 15, 2023

A calm emptiness prevails. Total vacation ahead: No folk dancing, no nothing—only HTML staring me in the face. And the idea of learning to code is a pleasant emptiness.

Free For What?

If I'll never play guitar for others, why maintain my playing skills? What is the purpose of playing guitar now that the audience is gone?

Not that I'm complaining. It's taken forty years, maybe more, to get rid of them. Thank God, they are finally gone! I love the openness and freedom this new emptiness gives me.

But my liberated mind, with its new open spaces, also allows me to ask: Free for what?

Advantages

Folk singing is just the opposite of classical guitar. I've never feared the audience and have had few, if any, thoughts about impressing them. But I do like pleasing them.

Folk dancing is the same way.

This is a soft, free day, and upcoming three-week vacation period. I wonder what new thoughts about my post-Covid career, direction, freedom, and attitude it will bring.

Wednesday, August 16, 2023
Avoidance and Distraction

I woke up with another horrible thought: Is expanding my "business" just a distraction? Am I pushing my tours, working on WordPress website, learning how to manage it, considering learning HTML and CSS code, as a distraction, all in order to avoid being an artist and creating books, folk dance choreography videos, and even some guitar (and reading) videos, and promoting them all?

Now that I'm at the pinnacle, am I falling off the ladder? Distracting myself instead of aiming and going higher?

Is it fear of effort? Maybe. Fear of failure? Somehow, strangely, I doubt it. In a way, I wish it were. Concrete fear of failure actually motivates me. But here I feel more of a vague deadness. Like I'm shutting something out, closing it down, but I don't know what. The artistic fountain of adventure and imagination?

Better to stick with the old fears of no money and keep chasing money, but in the "new" form of expanding my business.

Am I taking the "easy" way out by expanding my tours, business, and money making, distracting myself by following known, earthly roads? Am I also letting mortality haunt my mind, get in the way, as another distraction?

What about sacrifice? Today I realized that biblical sacrifices of animals, etc., are symbolic sacrifices of the ego and its parts, self-sacrifices so that one can focus on higher things. Am I sacrificing my art by distracting myself with business? No. Distraction is not a sacrifice. It is an *avoidance* of sacrifice! And, in the process, I am avoiding diving into the dangers of a higher calling.

Ugh, ugh, I hate to think this. But it could be true.

So is expanding my tour business the coward's way out? I'll make more money doing it. And I'll make less, even zero, creating my art. Or will I?

Truth is, my tour business is now in place, in order, as much as it needs to be. Maybe I am now ready to actually pursue my art! A grand hmm!

Thursday, August 17, 2023

It does feel like the beginning of a new era for me. The "Alhambra" crumbled, fell, with the advent of the video era. Now, working backward, I'm in a different guitar mood: a dynamic wake-up flow mood. The natural body path may be a fifteen-minute "warm-up."

I'm at the Moses stage. One video a day for one year, a get-it-out-there year. Folk dance videos, guitar videos, even reading and singing videos. Do it for personal reasons, to remember the stuff.

Distraction, and the Life Task of Artistic Creation

Death is so annoying. So is the fact I'm older, and will soon, or not so soon, eventually, die.

But hasn't this always been the case?

So death, and dwelling on it, are just another mental excuse, a distraction, like "business" and worrying about money. All are distractions from the focus on purpose, my life task: artistic creation! That is my purpose for this life, next life, all life.

Make it personal. Create a video record so I can remember. This leads to a new leaf. I'll call it: *One Year Artistic Creation Video Leaf.*

Make it personal, and make it good.

Accept that I'm older, and entering a next stage. Since all is flow and change, it's an illusion that I can preserve or even maintain anything. But I can step into the flow, become part of it, by creating flowing videos.

They may be remembered, or they may be forgotten. But so what? They are personal and made only for me in this life. They are my personal video library, shared by others, all the world, through YouTube.

I wanted another reason to make videos, a new attitude. Well, now I've got it. My videos will be "private" and personal, created only for me, and in my control. They are no longer made for public promotion, sales, and business. This although they will be shared by all through YouTube.

Friday, August 18, 2023
CEO Guitar

Mama Ring Finger takes her rightful leadership place.
As Mr. Brain CEO, I'm running the show.
Take a victor guitar lap.

CEO Folk Dance Tours

Miriam has confirmed and given me the key to my tours. They are indeed, folk dance tours. That is my niche, difference, and strength.

Offer folk dancing every day or night on every tour! Which means I need a folk dance teacher on every tour!

My new job as CEO is to find, train, and mentor others to do what I did: lead and teach folk dance on tours.

CEO *Trust and Verify*

As for my website, as CEO, is it better to learn to do it myself, or learn to trust others (experts) to do it for me? Of course, I must oversee and verify what they do, to make sure it's right.

A CEO is like a king running his domain. Like my new CEO job, the king's job is to oversee his domain, make sure things are running right.

Sunday, August 20, 2023

I like, want, and need a challenge. My knees, and body, maintenance of my temple (castle, instrument), are my challenge.

See this as an important "side" issue. "Side" because remembering that, through the mind and individual spirit, Spirit controls all. Focus on Spirit as the ultimate cure.

Interpreting *Shoftim* and the Torah: Make it personal. The ills of the body, along with their negative ideas, shall be cast out, stoned, and killed.

Three Furies

My three tremolo fingers are a bunch of spoiled brats, always fighting among themselves. They don't know how to work together. But if the Three Furies ever learn to coordinate their efforts, and work together, what a powerful team they will be!

Monday, August 21, 2023
Knees, Bookings, Returning to the World in Cooperstown, NY

See God in obstacles. Start with my knee(s). Bookings, too. Considering return to bookings. A new and next challenge: Can I stand, and deal with, functional nervousness, dive into material life?

Do bookings and knees go together?

If I did bookings, I sense I'd rise (definite), I might rise (doubt) above the challenge of my knees.

Should I play around with doubt in this manner? No. Truth is I know I would rise above it. Why? Because I would have to! The existence of others, my commitment and responsibility to serving them, which means performing, leading, and teaching them, would force me, command me, to rise above my worries and ills, and function. That's what work does. Forces me, pushes and commands me, to rise higher.

Sure by rejecting work, saying no to performing and bookings, I am deleting my nervousness, the unpleasantness of my fears. But I am also deleting my highs and victories. By turning down bookings, saying no to nervousness, I am living a gray cloud, free from fears and anxieties, which feels vaguely pleasant. But in reality, I'm living in a permanent cloud of defeat.

I wonder if this winless, victoryless life is reflected in knees going up and down Jacob's ladder stairs, and expressed through knee pain.

No question knee pain is an obstacle. But what, on a cosmic level, does it mean? And how can be handled, even cured?

Tuesday, August 22, 2023

I am under total TMS attack, including both legs and lower back. I can hardly walk.

I can't admit how much I am in conflict, actually hate, this so-called Cooperstown and Farm "vacation." Half of me doesn't, and didn't, want to leave the house, didn't want to leave my wonderful world of work and study; and the other half of me agrees with the first half. That makes a whole. All of me did not want to go on this vacation. And, in spite of that, due to family obligation, all of me went. And of course I didn't want to face my internal resistance. But it resisted anyway, and the war began, resulting in an almost crippling TMS attack. Every step hurt. I could hardly walk.

Today I recognize that the war is on. Yesterday I lost. Can I win today? Positive signs are that I'm totally conscious of the struggle, the war within me. There is no "real" pain. Only TMS. Crippling, awful, painful, debilitating, but ultimately, empty air, no physical damage, and, once the storm has passed, no mental damage either. Only the clear sky of awareness. And with awareness, the sun will shine.

Work Is Vacation, and Vice Versa

I may not want, or ever be able, to take a "vacation" again. In fact, post-Covid I've arranged it so that my work *is* my vacation, and vice versa. Always. On vacation I work, and when I work, I'm on vacation. No difference anymore.

Could failure to realize the maturing of the Vacation/Work, Work/Vacation life, and philosophy, be the cause of my TMS attack?

My new challenge, then: Somehow I have to combine both. It's okay to work on vacation. And even on vacation, with family all around me, it's okay to work—in fact, for me, it's good to work!

Somehow, my business is my life, and vice versa. Learn to accept and love it. Realize how fortunate (fortune/lucky, or destiny?) I am to have created such a fun, fulfilling, and profitable life and lifestyle.

How to make family past of my business, how to include them, even if only in my business thoughts and discussions, may be my next challenge, question, and step.

There is no relief from my work. Nor do I want relief, because I love it! Part of my resentment against "vacations" is that I hate leaving my work and the wonderful life it has created. Well, now I'm bringing I all with me on "vacation."

Will today's realizations dispel my TMS? If it is TMS, it should happen quickly, almost immediately. And it is TMS. Only doubt is its killer.

What about the heavy load of email responses?

Part of weight lifting: Weight training on the job.

(Weight training needs rests between lifts!)

TMS and Power

Hidden under the TMS legs is power! Fingers, too. Power is the ultimate fun! Is it the ultimate joy, too? Are they twins? Yes!

No-Doubt Land

In No-Doubt Land the opposites disappear.

Wednesday, August 23, 2023

On the farm. Playing guitar in my old room. Plus dwelling there. Meeting and playing with my old self. Fascinating.

Thursday, August 24, 2023

What's new?

1. Open morning with quick email scan? Check out the field?
2. Practice stairs. Up and down five times.
3. Knee bends (in bed) both directions.
4. "Alhambra" fast, smooth, and rolling. Cooked and done. Wonderful.

Imagine playing classical guitar for fun! Practically unheard of. . .until now. It started yesterday on the porch in back of the farm as I played the Flamencan dance "Zambra." Now to extend it to "Alhambra" and "Leyenda". . and on and on.

Imagine, and the idea was born on the little Jimmy farm.

CHAPTER THREE

The Book of AI

Friday, September 8, 2023
The Book of One

Al realized he liked to think. Although celestial thoughts were his best, his heavy, earthly ones weren't that bad either.

On the best days, all kinds swam freely in his head: good, bad, neutral, Albanian pizza topped with a Hungarian *csardas*, cheese dancing in a Budapest alley, ice cubes filled with Columbian radishes, it really didn't matter. Everything traveled harmoniously through space in a spicy, fun-floating way.

On his bad days, thoughts thudded—still and stiff, clunking and thrashing as they tumbled onto the floor of his brain, even reaching his amygdala, where they annoyed his excited, up-beat feelings, disturbing, even depressing, his peaceful state.

Ready to return. But to what?

Overthrow the old regime. This year's revolutionary task was now clear to him. How to uproot the destructive inner aspects of his old life? This is the New Year. The practice starts today.

Evil is a permanent force. So is good. The daily struggle between them is endless.

Awareness of this struggle is the first step.

Intention to defeat evil, and win, is the second.

Be specific: "Alhambra" was his first battlefield.

First playing on that battleground, ninety percent thumb brought out the melody while the other fingers sat at the edge, loving it. Ninety-six percent followed. Why did he need forty to fifty years to see something so obvious?

Here's the miracle idea: With Al Hambra released from prison and cured, could Knorbert the Knee follow? Or, as a guitar footstool, will he drop to three legs and tip over like a stool pigeon?

Al considered: could he be involved in creating such a miracle? With thumb released from prison, would the rest of the fingers follow?

Crossing the Excitement Line

Al pushed the Hambra. Such excitement. But did he have the energy, courage, and daring to cross the excitement line?

Of course he did.

Crossing the line was all so obvious now.

Al thought about Trump. "The man has the tickle of strong leadership. And he is funny. Like my thumb. The Trump thumb makes funny politics."

If it tickles me, it's an itch I like to scratch. Since I like to scratch, I will ask, Does scratching make it better or worse? I'd say better.

Is God funny? Well, why not? He has given me a good sense of humor, a funny thumb, and a fun-knee knee.

Can "Alhambra" be funny? Certainly, Al Hambra can. He's a fun-knee man. The Trump Thumb Meets Al Hambra. A good story.

A strong leader, excellent policies, and makes me laugh. What else do I need? Not much.

The biblical thought is the weighted squat.

Al said, "My thumb is out of prison. It's never going back!

"Such conscious defiance," fingers commented. "But what about us?"

"You guys can decide on your own. Trail me, dribble along,

stay back awhile if you like. Up to you. But I'm out of here. And truth is, if I'm out, you can't stay long."

Fingers crunched in silence as Al went on: "First thing I'll do when I hit the road is parade my proud defiance in front of everybody. It's Al Hambra Thumb Pride Day!"

Suddenly, he heard the sound of Knee crunching in the distance. Was it a grumble or a plea? Her tone divided in thirds, part plea, part grumble, and part philosophic: "If Thumb marches, can Knee Pride Day be far behind?"

Thumb softened a bit, bent toward her hobbling form, and gently explained, "If you can relax, open up, expand, and even bring fingers along, then. . . well. . .deep within, thumb and fingers, and even knees, are one."

Thumb paused, sucked his nail a bit, then went on. "Once pride is satisfied, expressed, released from prison, saturated with praise, once I pass through Pride's Gates and am intact, confident, and secure, then, yes, I'll bring my fingers along, and, if they work well (and I think they will), you're next."

Knee creaked with pleasure. "Oh, thank you, proud Thumb. I can't wait to join you. In the company of fingers, you'll be so hand-some. We'll be one big happy family playing guitar and dancing together."

"You're right, Knee. I like this freedom path, and walking with you will make it even better."

Al felt real good about this. He decided to build a new castle. He called it "Renew Al."

Saturday, September 9, 2023

I just heard that Yves Moreau died. Shocked, angry, scared, sad, I denied it, dazed. What now?

Mourn him, memorialize him, do his dances.

I'm annoyed that I have to take time off to think about death. I'm on a good path and don't want to change it. Death is another obstacle. A fearful, "ordinary" distraction, a sad annoyance.

How to handle it? It deserves respect, but do not cater to it. Say hello, mourn, move on, then mourn some more, and move on further.

Sunday, September 10, 2023

Toe-Ra Al, said, "The gift of life, all my dance steps, in fact all I have, comes from my brother Al Hambra. I'll always be grateful."

"Thanks, Toe-Ra, nice to hear." Al sipped his nectar. "Ma would be proud."

Al is Toe-Ra's tour agent and all-purpose guy. In the guitar world, he's Al Hambra. Even though Toe-Ra's father worked the Egypt sun god circuit, he was still a polytheistic kind of guy. So was his mother, but hardly anyone talks about her.

Toe-Ra Al combined polytheism and monotheism, melting Egypt into Israel, and did it all with one name.

Not bad for a guitarist.

And all was good before the revolt of the fingers. "We're important, too!" they cried, rising up to their full digital height.

"Knuckle down!" Al insisted using Mr. Abdomen to push his point. "Are you repeating or renewing yourself?" The wisdom and power of his shout scattered the fingers and strewed the notes they played across the desert. A complete disassembly—notes running wild, strangling any burning bush they could find, stretching the "Leyenda" barriers of humanity, traveling where no one had ever been before.

Moses gasped in amazement. "That's the best discovery and inspiration service a note can give," he declared.

The notes liked what they heard. They scurried back to listen. Thumb rolled in from the east: Al entered from the north. Moses held their attention while Al took out his Toe-Ra. Opening to page six, he called Index to point out a line. Ring, Middle, and Pinky followed. They stood together in a handsome formation. Then each digit pointed out its favorite note.

Al picked his favorite guitar out of the sky, and they all began to play "Recuerdos da la Alhambra."

Monday, September 11, 2023

Al said, "You're s smart cookie. But you are minimizing an important truth: You are worthy."

"Well, I don't know, Al. After all, although I'm reading the bible every day, trying to keep up with the orthodox. . .but, it's true, I do have a new take on it today."

"And what is that, my dear?"

"I'm seeing how it applies to me personally, how every morning I wake up to the same fight: Between polytheism and monotheism."

"Very lofty. How so?"

"Take my bad knee, for example. It hurts every morning. every day. What to do? I concluded: Stay on the path. What other choice is there? Plus the path may work."

"And, pray, what path is that?"

"The three-part walking path. Focusing on neck straight, abs in, legs relaxed and easy. Do it daily for an hour."

"Sounds good."

"I also kneel to alien gods, mainly the god of discouragement.

He visits me every morning. He often brings his god friends with their friendly fears, such as the god of old age, death, loneliness, abandonment, and fragility. I can't remember some of the others, there are so many. And I have to feed them, too."

Al nodded in agreement. "I understand. I have the same problem. Fly swatters are good, but it's hard to hit them all."

"Flies push me off the path."

"It's an affliction: my Battle of Wounded Knee every day."

Al then advised, "In these struggles, it's important to pit your bad knee against your good one."

"I don't have a good one. . . . Is there a good knee?"

"Of course. But it's hiding. Clouds of negative ions create abandonment. Bleak thoughts have scared her away."

"I agree. A little more light wouldn't hurt. But how do I get it into my knee?"

"Great question. Speak to Tom Thumb or Larry Finger. They may have answers."

Tuesday, September 12, 2023

Cancelling last night's folk dance class due to the storm revealed that my energy, effort, and love source is found in performing. And it doesn't even matter what medium I perform in: Guitar, singing, folk dancing, socializing, all are good.

The days of performing to "prove myself" are over. A positive view of performing would be a major and "final" post-Covid attitudinal shift.

"Alhambra" and Al are ready. The line between private and public has disintegrated. Group and individual are flowing into one another.

It's an easy transition, too.

Tell It to Al

"See people as energy packages," Al explained, "ready, willing, happy to explode and float their vibrational goodies everywhere for others to see, appreciate, and enjoy. A guitarist's fingers are like that, too."

I fell to my knees. Al pulled me up. "Ask like a man," he said.

I rose, squirmed, then pleaded in a virile manner, "Please be patient. I'll play slowly and carefully."

"No problem. I'll wait for you."

"Wait? That's no good. I want *love*. Love my playing, slow or fast."

"That's a tall order, son. Some folks will, most won't. But that's okay. The Wills is what you want."

"What if no one likes me? Suppose my audience walks out? Suppose it goes to zero."

"Zero is still an audience."

"It is?"

"Sure. It's called No Audience. (But even No still has Audience.) It's different. But No Audience is fun to play for, too."

"There's always an audience?"

"Yes."

"That doesn't makes me feel any better."

"Some day you might. Or you might not. The Audience doesn't care. And frankly, neither should you."

"I wish I was that strong."

Al considered the limits of power, then said, "I have a really good idea for you."

"What's that?

"Just play your guitar and shut up."

Thursday, September 14, 2023
Pure Performance

My guitar has been cleansed. Ready for pure performance.

Cleansed means the old, dried-up audience is gone, replaced by a new, vibrant, loving, accepting, patient and wonder-filled one. These folks all believe in miracles, renewal, rebirth, and the wonder of each day.

They have moved into my thumb. Now we pluck the strings together (total, תמם *tamam*).

Now Thumb is going out to play and have some fun. Let him roam, wild and free. It's a good start.

Re-interpret so-called stiffness; warm-up thigh "pain" as pleasure. Part of neural plasticity? Yes, I say.

Friday, September 15, 2023

Once warmed up with John Pavane, let Tom Thumb run wild. After he's gone wild for awhile, say twice), let fingers loose on the third run.

Sunday, September 17, 2023

Guitar:

Sor-fast. Al is no problem. Al fast and clear, too. Al fast clear. Bach G & R smooth and sweet. "Leyenda" crackling, too. Ley End A is now Leyen Da, the Chinese wonder, a Sino-Spanish alliance.

New characters with new names walking out of the guitar. It's a new world, a new whirl-d. Literal creations. (I'm literally creating them). . .along with YouTube Hubie.

Fiction is becoming reality, and vice versa. I'm making new friends late in life by giving birth to them, creating them from raw imagination. (Are all friends imaginary? With fiction as reality, and vice versa, the answer must be yes. Does the why of it really matter? No.)

Monday, September 18, 2023
Pure Curiosity: Abdominal Counting

Why play guitar? How about pure curiosity? How does playing this Bach piece work?

Today's discovery: Focusing on beats. Feel them in the stomach by tightening your abdominal muscles (slightly) on each beat.

Sor "Etude 12": 1 (First beat), "Alhambra": 2 and 3 (Second and third beat), "Leyenda": 1 (First beat).

Dynamic. Totally different.

But you need to have technical mastery, know the piece cold, before you can shift your attention to the abdominal stage.

Focusing on the beat, "abdominal counting," is very exciting, dynamic, satisfying, and the bottom line.

Tuesday, September 19, 2023
Creating a New Folk Dance Guitar Self and Vice Versa

My best ever "Alhambra" passed without incident. Beat with strong fingers. Clear and strong.

My "touch the string(s)–feel–pluck–listen" guitar practice method is successful.

Next step: How to apply it to my dance body?

First, how does it work? For guitar, starting with the Covid sabbatical break, I cleared the pressure to perform, make money playing professionally, and the never-ending internal pressure to some day, even years away, give concerts. Slowly, inch by inch, I cleared my brain, cleansing every corner, power-washing into oblivion every negative miserable thought, and finally, creating a *tabula rasa*. With all debris cleared, the seed of a new guitar-playing self could be planted. As I accustomed myself to living in a wide open field, this guitar self seed sprouted, and a healthy, strong baby emerged, happy, smiling, and laughing under the sun.

On to my body. How to remove its folk dance pressures. First is to admit it *creates* pressure.

How so? Even though I enjoy teaching and leading this low financial reward profession, it still creates pressure, even if it is only having to show up for the job. And after that, I still have to put on a good show, do a *good* job.

Can I perform without the pressure to do a good job? At the moment, I doubt it.

What is performing but an appearance?

Appearing is easy: just be there. But when you appear as a performer, folks expect you to create something on the spot. And you agree, since you have chosen to appear. You have also chosen to be pressured.

Paradoxically, if you can choose to be pressured, can you also choose not to be?

To stand in front of others without obligation, a free being, and, as performer, not perform? Can you choose nothing while others wait around expecting something?

Can you choose to disappoint them?

Or think that "disappointment" will be an elevation in disguise?

Lots of good questions.

Turning guitar self into folk dance self: Another path begins.

Thursday, September 21, 2023
Grateful for My Problems: Fix Them

The malfunction of my tour registration forms threatens my business and financial survival at its core. It scares and upsets me; I'm a bit frantic. Fix this immediately. My business isn't right.

What can I do? Expect things will go wrong! Then expect to fix them! As humans, our job is repairing the world. To fix things is exactly right. So the fact my tour registration forms are broken and I must fix them, although annoying, is correct.

Gratefulness for my tour problem is a better attitude. To exchange anger, frustration, sadness, and annoyance for gratefulness would be wonderful. How to develop and sustain such an attitude? That is my question and challenge!

Friday, September 22, 2023
Slow Power

Acknowledge, then express, the wolf as it howls and twists slowly inside my mind. Say hello to its slow movement and the grumbles of its quiet power.

Slow-soft grows, hidden, private, and safe, gradually transforming into a public performance, loud and screaming.

Meet Mr. Slow. He's been oppressed, down, living in the basement so many years. But he's coming up the stairs, greeting the sunlight.

Guitar in the Legs

When I bent forward in a hamstring stretch this morning, I felt guitar in the legs. It's the first time.

Imagine, folk dance guitar in my legs and yogic body.

Saturday, September 23, 2023
Unsolved Problems

I have a problem-filled life—and that is good!

Problems are my middle name.

Today's it's the new iPhone 12. How to work the damn thing?

Then live happily, thankfully, and gratefully with unsolved problems?

Sunday, September 24, 2023
Forever Is The Way To Go: Let the Wahoo Currents Flow

I'm high from website button-creation victory. I also have a touch of sore throat. I rested yesterday. Why now?

Fearing, humbled, and sick made a sudden return. I deserve to be down because of my high success. My wrathful Lord Mother appeared. "Don't you dare! Don't you dare step out of the old neighborhood. Effort, trying, success—harmful and evil. The punishment of sickness upon you. Here's a sore throat, and more to come! Too much success. Bad, bad, bad. You've defeated Death itself. Such hubris! Remember your place! Low among the weeds."

Well, Mother Wrath, for me, great successes have been rare. In fact, this was my first Wahoo in months, maybe years, maybe since Covid. I loved it!

"So, in spite of warnings and possible wrathful vengeance, I'm going to milk the joy of yesterday's button-creation victory. From now on, I'm looking for more Wahoos. I want to fill the days I have left in this temporal life with them."

Temporal? How sad and realistic.

Or is it?

Temporal knowledge is the cure for hubris.

Living is fleeting, but Life is everlasting. I like this long-term view. So goodbye Wrathful Lord Mother, at least for today.

Monday, September 25, 2023
Slow Wisdom

I'm reading the Torah in Hebrew, and moving slower, much slower. Maybe only a sentence, even a new word, a day.

It's disappointing to read so slowly. What's the matter with my brain? On one level, my ego and formerly youthful cognitive apparatus is being threatened; on the other hand, reading slowly creates maturity, deepening, and wisdom.

Presently, things are moving more slowly in my mind and life: slow Torah, slow guitar, slow yoga, slow focus. Not a bad thing, only different.

Dropping the Ego: Ego Goodbye

I'm adding Milan's "Pavane in A" to my morning guitar. I'm playing its formerly fast scale passage slower, egoless, and laden with wisdom. Am I willing to drop my ego for the wiser good? Is that my next direction? Sadly and happily, yes. I'm sad to lose it but happy to be wiser. In fact, the whole slow and fast controversy, giving a concert, playing well or not, is about ego.

Ego is a good thing to lose, or give up, at least for awhile.

Dear Alicia,
Thanks for your email and question.
I am delighted that "De Boca Del Dyo" is a favorite in the San Francisco Bay Area, and I appreciate your telling me.

I've attached folk dance instructions and the YouTube link: "De Boka Del Dyo." More information can be found in my book of folk dance choreographies, A Treasury of International Folk Dances, *available on Amazon.*

As I see it, "De Boca" is religious dance of worship in the Jewish Ladino Sephardic tradition. The song was written in Ladino by the Ladino singer Flory Jagoda of Sarajevo. It is a prayer and I choreographed it with that in mind.

To my knowledge, shimmies are not in the Jewish Bosnian Ladino folk dance tradition (especially in prayer or worship dances), so I did not add any to the dance. My answer is, "No shimmies."

Of course, folk dancing also has a tradition of artistic freedom, so, on another level, folk dancers can add or subtract whatever they want. But according to my vision, and to keep in the spirit of Flory Jagoda's music, "De Boca Del Dyo" (From the Mouth of God) has no shimmies.

Lots of luck, and keep dancing!

Jim

P.S. You asked such an interesting question. Would you mind if I sent your letter, along with my answer to folk dance magazines? How to dance and choreograph are such fascinating topics. I think folk dancers will want to know these thoughts.

Wednesday, September 27, 2023
Going All the Way

I've always been a believer. The only question is can I, will I, go all the way. The only answer can be: Yes.

Since depression and fear twist my mind, how can I trust my market decisions? Truth is, I can't. This is my flaw, my temptation. When the market is good, I jump in; when it's bad, I jump out. I do just the opposite of what I should do. I do the wrong thing, and I always do. And I have done it for years.

The only "good" and productive way for me is to get out of trading completely.

Can I do such a thing, especially when the market goes up? Temptation again, with its false promises of trading stocks and its instant wealth.

Money is my weakness and Achilles heel—my hope of a false heaven and false Lord support, bestowing sudden protective wealth and happiness upon me.

To not return to trading is my biblical challenge. My positive exchange with this deal is to be, and become, more productive. Put the money into the bank, bonds, or interest bearing stuff. Let the erudition flow: A positive gift

Close the trading gates: A positive gift as well. Mr. Higher Up always said no, as witness my losing money and constant failure over the years. But due to ego, I refused to listen. So why am I listening now? I am ready. To unleash my erudition and love and learning. Love of learning results in erudition.

No longer hiding or apologizing, through humor and fantasy fiction, for my love of learning and erudition. Jewish, Talmudic they are. Of course, other traditions have it, too, but despite a secular uporinging, Jewish roots are in my soul.

Fear of jumping into the "Alhambra" shows lack of faith in God. Can I practice faith by practicing jumping right in? Will God carry me on His eagle wings? According to Judaism, with complete faith, yes.

Thursday, September 28, 2023

The Beat is my security and support system. Dive in. Dopamine shall reign. Thumb and knee will follow.

The "Sor Etude Number 12" spoke to me: "Push yourself until you are crazy. Repeat, repeat, repeat, over, over, and over and over, and then repeat some more. Repeat until you pop, sizzle, and break the limits. Then great satisfaction occurs."

"Thanks, Etude," I said. "You're a good guy."

Then I gave it a shot. First came frantic, followed by chaotic, empty, and falling. "It's okay," said Etude by way of encouragement. "You're taking the chance, diving in."

"It's scary."

"So what? Just keep going. There's glory up ahead."

"Okay, okay. . . not yet, not yet. . . my fingers are loosening . . .now they're starting to fly."

"Keep at it. Flying fingers create the porridge. The eagle soars. Glory is coming."

"I love it. What's the next step?"

"Make it common."

Height is destiny; weight is free will. Life is a combo. Change your karma. Knee is also free will. I changed Al Hambra. Now for Knee.

Can arthritis be reversed? I'm betting on yes.

Friday, September 29, 2023

Al spoke: "A new softness is emerging in my 'Milan Pavane in C,' mostly expressed in and through the ring finger—marriage, feminine. Emergence of the ring finger: a soft, non-push power.

"Can I see a Pavane? Faith would be a good start. Dive into

the sales process. Forget results.

"I could practice strong fingers until I get it out of my system. But why would I do that? After all, fast strong fingers have their own exhilaration. The sensual fluid of finger joy runs through the fingertips. And sometimes even more when you pluck loud and fast. Can't stay in this state of glory very long, but its government is memorable. In fact, diving into almost anything brings exhilaration. But you have to break barriers first. And every day brings a new barrier."

Saturday, September 30, 2023
Preparing for Eternity: Preparing for the Eternal Audience

Al said, "I'm playing guitar for the eternal audience. Always have and always will. Long term, that's the only truth. It's not called the eternal for nothing. The audience is always there and lasts forever.

"Once you stop complaining about transience, the cloud passes.

"As for the contemporary audience, the human form looks pretty real. On the other hand, how real can you be if you're transient? Look at other folks with a grain of salt, or at least of sand. Fleshy forms flip and flop, blown about by desert winds, whittled and whacked by ocean waves.

"It's the end of the year, end of Torah reading, end of Moses. I'm preparing for eternity. So is everyone else. We're all in it together. I'm so sad to see my friend, a great leader, die alone on Mt. Nebo. Was he lonely? I doubt it. Isolated, he still had good company. Always had.

"The sadness problem never disappears but lurks in the background, periodically slipping out of dark alleys into the foreground. What to do? Just cry and watch the clouds pass.

"Meanwhile, I'll stand out, isolate myself, and protrude like a mountain. Are mountains sad? I'll ask next one I meet.

"I watched old folk dance and tour videos last night, surprised at how good they were. Upload them to YouTube? But they're old. Will people appreciate them?

"Of course, I could sneak them into eternity by uploading them and not telling anyone. No one would know.

"On the other hand, eternity includes the present. Why *not* tell the living? Announce, market, and publicize these ancient jewels. Playing and dancing for my ancestors, children of the future, and the transient aspects of present folks is a good thing. How can it be bad? Only embarrassing. But in eternity, even that will be forgotten.

"Once you stop complaining about time and dive into now, the clouds pass. Complaints and cries turn into a good laugh."

Sunday, October 1, 2023
All Good Stuff

Al Hambra spoke: "Tooth implants will plant a new strength into my mouth. But the process hurts so much. I'd like my pain to have some cosmic significance, be more meaningful. Suffering is better if it has a reason. Otherwise, it's just a waste.

"So what's the reason? Just as a musician needs a good instrument, I need a good body if I am to play my cosmic song well. Tooth implants improve the instrument and so, are a worthy cause. I'll eat better, look better. I'll profit and so will others. No wasted suffering. More love will be spread around. Good stuff.

"My guitar playing is about implanting love, about healing myself and others. Feeling and expressing it through each note, and on all levels, connects my eternal audience with the present one. All good stuff."

Monday, October 2, 2023

Al said: "Love in 'Alhambra' starts in the bass. But it doesn't end there."

Get love (eternity) into my life. Or let love into my life?
"Get" means it comes from outside; "let" means it comes from within. (And if the deed has no love in it, it's a waste of time.)
How can I put some love into my tours? I know where the motivation for financial profit is. But where is the love? I know they go together, along with the Magnificence. Are love and eternity the same?
Love is eternity, yes, and vice versa.

Index finger points to shining, explodes with sizzle and break-out light. High energy fire is an aspect of its love. Fire and love fuse in focus.

Tuesday, October 3, 2023
Remember the River: Leading the Half-Mind Life

Al said, "I can't transfer my contacts and videos from my PC to my new iPhone 12, plus the email doesn't work. It's a mess. I hate messes. When things go wrong, I'm annoyed, even scared.

"I don't like these feelings. Is there a better way of approaching the bothers of this world? Yes. Welcome them as challenges. Be happy that now my mind can be occupied with something that will improve my life. Also, without problems, an empty mind creates its own problems. Nature abhors a vacuum. To fill it, I'd invent something to do, a new challenge. So why not be grateful for the ones I have?

"Keep part of my mind on the big picture. Beneath all these problems, the flow continues. Stay in the flow. Keep half my mind in the River as I swim toward shore."

Love Your Enemy

Might as well learn to love your enemy since he or she will always be there. Fighting them is an endless struggle. Although peace does happen, new enemies emerge. So keep fighting. To lower frustration and suffering level, keep love going in the process.

CHAPTER FOUR

Leadership: New Stuff

Wednesday, October 4, 2023

To express Torah through guitar is a wonderful thing. But don't tell anyone. It's a secret, a non-verbal communication.

Friday, October 6, 2023
Land of Tabula Rasa

Back to emptiness. Clear the slate, wipe out the past, start over. Play guitar softly. (But not necessarily slowly.)

Soft signifies secret, inward, hidden. The audience can't hear it unless they make an effort (and really want to). Soft means the mind is free, and the imagination can run wild—and does.

Soft playing leads to the Garden of Eden.

Happy Warrior

Since life is a battle between good and evil, why not wake up fighting, ready for it?

I have control of my attitude. When I wake up, I can choose up, down, happy, sad, resistant, or reluctant.

Monday, October 9, 2023

Why not choose happy? Play guitar as a happy warrior.

If I played as a happy warrior, I would fight evil by being a pro-good advocate. Then I would employ my special finger forces: fast, strong, and light.

Vladimir Horowitz was right: Repetition and neuro-plasticity: Change my physical structure through massive repetitions.

Be Kind To Fingers Fiction Week

Maybe my journal will evolve into a fiction.

Soft guitar playing leads to the power of gentle. Gentle makes others willing to give. With soft leading to gentle, I play "Alhambra" on the first shot! Soft brings gentle brings kind brings power.

Can I be gentle with myself? It all starts with me. Being kind to my fingers brings kindness to "Alhambra." Kindness paradoxically gives me a great new kind of power. Note the etymology: "Kind" is related to "kin," related to family, related to Latin *gen*, related to indigenous people, related to "genus" (birth), and thus family. I'm playing guitar with my finger family—and it is fun! I can even roughhouse with them, which means playing hard and loud with them. And this is even more fun!

I found this through the fiction of fingers and the finger family. Fiction is indigenous indirection.

Tuesday, October 10, 2023
Bored With Fear

Last night was the first time I taught folk dancing without fear. No pre-performance anxiety. Gone. Disappeared. Will this overflow into guitar? I want that.

Am I getting bored with fear? It's been so many years. Maybe my time has come. Without fear, what will stimulate and motivate me now? Yet even this motivation question is becoming boring.

Even the desire to celebrate this fearless idea (fact?) is over. It's just a fact. Steady, even, calm. I'm getting ready to step into the land beyond bored.

All this happened after tooth-implant pain and new-computer confusion. Perhaps the whole process symbolizes implanting a new mode of existence.

Saturday, October 14, 2423
Building A Foundation

Maybe guitar and a strong "Alhambra" tremolo are just the necessary groundwork for confidence and building a foundation— plus a strong body through yoga, exercise, weights, and dance.

Foundation for what?

Are folk dance and tours my only weapon? I doubt it.

What about the books I've written? Could I ever "unleash" them with a good show of promotion and sales?

Are my books good for people? Will they help them? Should people spend time and thought with them? In other words, do I believe in them and their importance and power enough to put in the effort of promoting and selling them? An old question, sure, but one I am ready to return to.

Is the foundation I'm really talking about a confidence foundation? Confidence in my books? The inability to sell them is a big frustration in my life. It is the one thing I want but have not done. I hate admitting it. In fact, I can feel my stomach turning as I do. I am afraid to push out my inner, deeper, creative, artistic self.

Guitar and Book Sales

"Pavane in C": The slow, stately march of my books out of the closet through the court, and into the public square of my formerly medieval, but now renaissance, village.

Yes, I have been hiding my book self behind the guitar, partly because I had to make a living. But those days are over.

It will take an "elevated view" of myself to pull it off. Is this "elevated view" the real one, the Moses view? Moses said he couldn't do it alone but needed God's help, so God made him His spokesman. No question I could use some help in this area, too.

Sunday, October 15, 2023
Making the Maximum Effort: Fun and Glory in a Nutshell

A bit at loose ends this morning. I have lost or forgotten my purpose. I know what's right and good for me. So I need to use my will and force myself to follow my miracle schedule. Just shut up and do it.

They say meditation is good to do every day. Well, my schedule is my meditation practice, my personal way of worship. That's why I feel lost, abandoned, and upset without it. Truth is, most days I follow my practice. Today will be no exception.

My meditations are all solitary things. My four forms—study, writing, guitar, and exercise, are all done alone. solo. Evidently, quiet and separate are the best way I can concentrate on, touch, and remember my juice connection. It is also why business is never part of it.

Break: Lots of crying over the death of Moses. Add me, my wife, all those around me. Crying, mourning, is the only way to get through the tunnel. Just do it. Maybe every morning. First you cry, then you laugh. To paraphrase Kahlil Gibran: Tears and laughter are twins in life.

I need business, too. It is really the fifth spoke of the schedule wheel. I apply the skills and talents I discover and develop during meditation, to work with and affect others, and heal the world. (Meditation is half , business the other half: Combined they equal one whole.)

Business is about service to others; socializing is about living with others (from Latin *socius*: "companionship").

In my mind, the phrase "service to others" has the feeling of separation, of "I and them," performing something for them. Socializing, on the other hand, has more of "me with them," all of us together, no individual performing a service. In a social situation, role and ego merge with others. There's a loss, giving up, of identity; ego is less important.

My skills and talents are not needed to socialize. I can perform nothing, do nothing, be nothing, and still be with others. All I need is to show up.

Monday, October 16, 2023

The battle is ever between two worlds: light and dark, heaven and hell, good and evil, energy and inertia, flesh and spirit, audience and solo, public and private, community and individual. Give each on its due.

J. S. Bach said he composed music for the glory of God.

Why not play guitar for the same reason?

Go deep within to find the center. Play for the melt-down glory of Magnificence. The audience can sit in the circle of radiance and listen, if it likes.

The past two weeks of tooth and computer problems have broken my upward momentum. Hard to get back on track. But what track? So far the only good thing coming out of this dark two-week tunnel is my guitar playing.

Is a new implant base being built starting with my guitar?

Note: No videos involved. No tours, folk dance, or sales either. Have I been misled? Fooled? Are guitar and music my real foundation?

Tooth implants will implant a new bite into my life! New seed creates a new root, and a new plant will flower. Base it, not on videos, but on guitar and music. Pulling away from computer, tours, business, and money to find my essence.

Can I live within my essence without them? Suppose I gave them up for a week and lived in guitar and music.

Tuesday, October 17, 2023

A strange and awesome place: words nobody knows but every scholar speculates upon.

Skip around the Torah, play guitar for Al and the Magnificence. Yes, everyone writes their own bible.

I touched it for a quarter of a second, the awesome place where I would not fear death because I am part of eternal life. That's what Al is all about: The quest for eternal life.

Wednesday, October 18, 2023

My email isn't working this morning. I'm frustrated. Why is this happening to me now?

Why do I interpret frustration as a personal attack?

I'd rather see obstacles as hidden opportunities for growth, development, and expansion. But so far, I don't. But attitude is up to me. I could choose to reinterpret frustration, redefine it as today's battle, my daily struggle for survival. Thus, would I turn a negative twist into a positive. No one decides I'm a victim but me.

I'll do it. A post-monastery, post-Covid attitude change and re-entry into society.

The Guitar Finger Story of Handsome Hand

My ring finger is tonally tough—strong, hard, and naily. She reminds me of power.

Do not fight her nailiness. Dive into it. Naily is your friend.

She also teaches how to deal with stymie in her Frustration One class. "Use a combo of tough and hard, sprinkled with love," she says. "Fight frustration with nail power."

My index finger points the way. He's full of purpose

Middle finger mediates between index and ring. During the Grand Gender Compromise of 2017, middle finger traded "he" and "she" for "it." Today it remains sexless, gender-free, but quite smart.

When my ring finger is straightened, raised, or in use, she is powerful. I often use her strength to deal with frustration. Then I consult with index for direction and purpose. The obvious mediation between these two is performed by middle finger.

My right hand combination of purpose, power, and mediation is a handsome hand. Listeners love it.

Thumb watches me while all the fingers smile.

And pinky? Where does she fit in? Pinky's the stand-up comedian supplying humor and good laugh.

Thursday, October 19, 2023
Art Can Heal the World

Why not play guitar to heal the world? And folk dance, too. This could be my contribution to politics. The artistic healing of the world through thoughts of art.

Fast, fun, joy, exhilaration—dancing *kopanitsa* on the road to the healing life. Speed and excitement go together. Create the trance of folk dance.

Healing through exhilaration is what fast is all about.

As for guitar, touch lightly, and you can calm the soul.

Friday, October 20, 2023
Guitar Warm-Up

Focus my first opening thought: I have exhilaration at my finger tips! (Not speed, not fast, not slow, but exhilaration.)

Spread it through all my guitar pieces. This is my goal, the apotheosis of a different way thinking and practice.

Get the Exhilaration Team in order. The A Team, Alhambra Tremolo Team, and it has to stay in order all day! The Team, although universal in idea and scope, is ethnically Spanish, its members all from Spain. Diego Annularis comes from Madrid; Madre Medius was born in Granada but now lives in Cadiz; Jimenez Indice, originally from Santiago de Compostela, moved to Malaga for its warm weather and beaches.

This E Team, organized and ruled by Rolando Thumb, aka "The Supreme," always threatens: "Better work together, or else!" Along with consultant Alberto Rocco (Ein Stein), they discovered the success formula $E=MC^2$, always insisting on daily exhilaration practice.

Sunday, October 22, 2023
The New Nihilism

Old stuff in a new bottle. Blurring distinctions leads to confused thinking, leads to destruction and nihilism. Good versus evil.

I'm dealing with hassles; this time it's PayPal. How does this fucker work? I can lose everything I own and love in one moment. Deal with it? How?

Once everything is destroyed—including me—what is left? Only the Vibration. Evidently, the Vibration can never be destroyed ($E=MC^2$). How do I contact and stay connected to exhilaration! Follow the sanity and sanctity of practice.

Monday, October 23, 2023
History Period

Can I combine history with guitar?
How would Ashurbanipal play Sor's "Etude Number 12"?

Tuesday, October 24, 2023

I'm becoming a biblical, emotional, artistic scholar. Is there such a thing? Where do I fit into history? Where does it fit into me? How do I connect and not be alone?

Back to school. Could I actually be a scholar? Yes, but I must be an emotional, artistic one. Not the dry, unfeeling, "intellectual" scholars I picture from the past.

My kind of scholarship must be exciting, adventurous, emotional, dynamic, and artistic.

Maybe it always was, and I merely thought it was dry to protect myself from my love and emotions, and from the secret, and not-so-secret, inferiority complex blanketing my being—manifested so clearly in guitar, study, and intellect.

But through "Alhambra" salvation, the guitar complex has dribbled away, being transformed and cured.   Now it's time to apply the "Alhambra" cure to the intellect. Almost no sooner said than done.

Just as Pavane Power is coursing through my veins via the wrist portal so I shall apply this flow to scholarship.

Wednesday, October 25, 2023
Babylonian Guitar

The Amorites displaced the Sumerians, founded Babylonia, spoke Akkadian, and ruled from 2,100 to 1,700 BC. Then as

Hyksos, they invaded and ruled Egypt in the 1700 BC.

Play guitar like a Babylonian Amorite. Speak and sing in Akkadian. Amorite children play on the grass-green lawn, shout, squeal, and laugh, playing Sor "Etude Number 12": They run light and fast. Crack their code, swift, light, and silent.

Establish the right hand rule of Hammurabic law.

Play the Akkadian "Alhambra."

Establish Hammurabic thumb dominance. It works.

Thursday, October 26, 2023

After so much frustration trying to fix it, my PayPal account finally works! I won. I'm so happy! All my work with its frustration, anger, impotence, and impatience paid off. I can't believe it. Deal with the feeling of glorious happiness.

Guitar History

True guitar playing began during the stone age. Neolithic rock groups like "Nathan and the Stoned Sediments" and "Pete Paleolithic and his Peters" dominated the pre-Europe music scene. (They say Pleistcenomorphic Paul, Pete's greatest of grandfathers, had been a Cenozoic rock star.)

Later, with the discovery of copper, "Carol's Chalcolithic Kurls" took the Mount Carmel Tel scene by storm. Using a light copper touch, her musico-speleologic fame lasted well into the Bronze age.

Of course, Phil Philistine, aka "Land-Phil," practicing for years on beaches of the Gaza coast before ploughing, sling shot and base guitar in hand, to wipe out "Goliath and the Punics," aka "Punies," above Tel Igneous.

Did Neolithic players have footstools hidden in their caves? Were they ever used? Or was their playing style merely phlamenco?

Recently, fragments of the Pulgaromics Scroll, with essays on the economic power of the Stone Age thumb, were discovered both in the Qumran caves as well as a neolithic suburb near Altimara in northern Spain. Some Pleistocene teachers taught an ancient doctrine: *Finger families cannot be separated.* All digits stick together, no matter what. This iron-clad rule, which knocked out Chalco and Bronze Age separatists, has remained in tradition right up to the present.

How strange: I'm too happy to work. It feels like things are falling into place for the first time in weeks. The PayPal success is lighting my day. Would even more financial stability make me even happier? To know every corner of my financial situation.

Friday, October 27, 2023
Slow Power

I love the stable, steady power of the slow, meaty, majestic, gorgeous tremolo. Can such a thing fit into the world?

The acceptance—even the glory—of slow power is worth considering.

Two styles of strength: fast as a rabbit, speed power; powerful as a bull, slow power. Both have their place. This end-of-the-road acceptance is wisdom at its best.

How will slow power—and the glory of it—affect my email and Email Merge study? And editing, and the overwhelmed feeling?

Slow power dissolves impatience. It glorifies faith in commitment, perseverance, steady work, and sticking to it. It expresses the faith that I can solve my problems.

Yes, there are very good things I can find in slowness.

Saturday, October 28, 2023
The Tyranny of Technique Is Over

Talking about bible, music, and folk dancing, among other things, wipes away the magic and mystery. An ineffable treasure.

Acceptance of slow power completes the cycle.

My First Audience

Adam and Eve listen intently to my slow power guitar (and violin) playing in the Garden of Eden. They are my first audience, listening with awe, wonder, innocence, and amazement, babies in adult clothing.

Love my new audience. Fast or slow, they don't care.

The laughing and laughable level of Sor's "Etude Number 12" played at super speed. Ridiculous, crazy, mucho fun!

Start "Alhambra" on that level. What happens? Ridiculous and crazy become normal. Mucho fun is normalized, and I move up. It takes years for the gates to open. But once they do, the water flows through immediately and very fast!

Sunday, October 29, 2023
Strong and Comfortable Is the New Normal

Annularis ("a") finger introduced its strength. My tremolo is all even now.

So with all guitar barriers down, where do I go from here?

Once warmed up, begin wild and crazy, loose and warm. Let

this become the new normal.

"Alhambra" sails on at a strong, comfortable pace. And it starts with guitar but doesn't end there.

It's All So Clear

It's all so clear: Evil has to be defeated; good has to win. There can be no compromise. It's win or lose, period. The battle takes place within each person, then moves from there into society, politics, diplomacy, and, if not dealt with and settled there, physical war.

The good has to be constantly maintained, the evil constantly beaten back. The battle between good and evil goes on forever.

So where do you start? The only place you have control of: yourself. From there, results spread out to others. Look within. Amazing what you will find.

Wild Sales Alhambra Campaign

Next challenge: Making emails fun!

I will learn Email Merge, canva.com, making videos, using YouTube videos, all in the process of creating these email ads. I'll throw in writing, the website, and all my other skills: one grand smorgasbord of skills applied to sales. And I'll put these ads on Facebook, too.

"A" is the letter of the solidified, stable and strong, post-Covid, new normal life. It stands for All, "Alhambra," Ads, A-team, and Amore.

No more separation. All skills thrown into one grand email sales pot dancing together creating the Wild Sales/ Alhambra All Is One campaign.

Creating Fun

I like the phrase "create fun." In fact, I like it much better than "having" fun. "Having fun" implies that fun is given to you from the outside, like a present. You have little to no control over it. "Creating fun" puts it entirely in your hands. In addition you get "created in the image of God," Garden of Eden, Michelangelo, artistry.

Parents tell their children, "Go out and play. Have fun." You can have this apple, you can have fun. Permission and freedom comes from them as a reward, a gift. The freedom to have fun comes from them, not their kids.

Children have fun.

Adults create fun.

Monday, October 30, 2023

God bless clarity—and the sharp line between good and evil.

Inject creative fun into existential misery. Put humor and crazy fantasy into the dark clouds overhead, and watch them pass. Consciously, use will power to take the sores out of my Fernando Sor "Etude Number 12." Add the Pavane in Sea (C Pavane) fun-ny (knee) dance.

Ferdinand and the Light Touch

"I want to be big and strong," little Ferdinand complained on his sixth birthday as he stared across the Mediterranean from his family's Malaga apartment high on the hill. The sun burned the Spanish beaches on that cloudless July day.

His uncle, the great and wise Alberto Una Rocca, born in Arbeiter Auf Rhinestein, Bavaria, answered at the speed of light,

"That's easy. Start off with a light touch."

"What?"

"A light touch, with both your right and left hand. That will create happiness quickly. In fact, with a light touch you can travel at the speed of light."

"Slow down, Uncle. You talk so fast I can't understand a word."

Alberto repeated his wisdom slowly. Freddie's eyes lit up. "Ah, now I see, 'C,' or 'sea.' But how will going faster make me taller?"

"Easy. Tall and fast are the same thing. It's just a matter of seeing, C-ing, or seaing it that way."

"I sea."

"Indeed, you do. C-ing used to belong to a mere *pavane,* but now, using the light-touch method, everything that used to be two- or even three, or more, creating division, frustration, anger, misery, even hate—is now one. They and them become we and us. Energy equals Me and C squared."

"Uncle Alberto, Mommy say that you are a genius."

"It's true. But so are you. You just have to see, C, sea it that way. But now, as your favorite uncle, I'm giving it, passing the genie of my genius, on to you. So from now on, it's geni-Us."

Then both geniuses put on their bathing suits and walked down to the Malaga beach for a cool dip in the Mediterranean see, C, sea.

Years later, when Freddie played guitar, he asked his uncle: "How can I have a sense of humor and have fun with the things I do, when I only see dark clouds above?"

"Easy," answered Uncle Alberto. "Force yourself. Use your will power to focus. When those dark clouds pass, or the serpent of gloom, doom, and evil raises its head, fight it hard. Don't give an inch. As soon as its poisonous head pops up, crush and destroy it. Have no mercy. If you don't kill it, it will kill you."

"But dear uncle, isn't that rather harsh? You know that, after growing up with Aunt Dolores, and other dismembers of my family, I can handle any snake."

"Ah, but you must learn to distinguish one snake from another. Those snakes you're thinking of love you and only want good things for you. They only *look* like snakes. The real ones often hide in your basement, slither away and disappear as soon as you see them. They're smart, but don't be fooled."

"How can I distinguish good from bad?"

"Easy. You're a guitar player. A clear tremolo is always on the side of goodness. Beware of the *uneven* tremolo. Keep practicing. Aim for clarity. An uneven tremolo is fickle and leans toward evil. It must be eradicated through deep finger and wrist relaxation, which leads to lightness, light, and infinite power. Keep practicing. Trading in evil for good is an unbeatable deal."

"You're right, Uncle. When my tremolo is even, it feels so pleasant and real."

Tuesday, October 31, 2023
The Creative Path

Must I be creative every day?

Aside from rest and sleep, what else is there to do?

Basically, nothing. So there's no real choice; it's creative or else. So just shut up and do it. My path is right.

Even under the black cloud, I can create my way out of darkness. Between rounds lie fatigue, rest, and sleep. Not bad places to be. Plus, in those *ki tov/hineh tov* moments, I can relish the *aaah* of satisfaction after a job well done. If it's good enough for Him, it's good enough for me.

So roll on. Someday is today; the creative moment is now.

How will little Freddie Sor play his "Number 12"? Like a six-year-old? Older? So young is he, a mere child. What used to matter at six, at twelve doesn't matter any more. The biblical Lot veil has lifted, exposing childhood.

Freddie and his friend Al (Hambra) sit on the living room floor, playing with their blocks. And that's enough. Any other friends to invite? Maybe Johnny Bach from next door.

Very self-contained, Freddie feels liberated. How to fill the void of freedom?

Create a house, another note, a fresh song, plant flowers in the ditch. Make a *ki tov* moment. The garden road is open.

Wednesday, November 1, 2023
Expressing and Expanding the Good

The pro-Hamas (so-called pro-Palestine) marches around the world and especially in this country totally disgust and enrage me. As we border on World War III, the final showdown between good and evil, between woke and the woken, is here.

What can, will, or must I do about it? If anything?

The only thing I can think of, something I might actually do, commit myself to, is keep studying. Torah and more.

Can I study harder, make a bigger commitment? Am I at maximum?

Here is my strange but astonishing conclusion: Retreat harder (into self) and study harder. That is my "method" of fighting the war.

Retreat hardens, toughens the inner core of resistance, rebellion, and creates explosives of dynamite and dynamism in its wake. I retreat through the tunnel to my cave in order to create new explosives and powers to fight. Mine is a quiet, persistent, unending resistance and rebellion against evil. I never give up. I dive further within, creating more steel and iron, hardening my core, toughening the good, recognizing and rebelling against evil tendencies both within and without. Then, when and where the right time comes, I use my skills and powers to fight the war.

How is this fighting self, hardened core of purpose, expressed? Through the arts. My guitar, writing, dancing, even tours and business, are about expressing and expanding the good. And this is something I can and will do.

First, feel and know the good. Then work to express and expanding it.

Specifically, how is this done?

Guitar: With each note think of expressing and expanding the good. Then add this idea to everything I do.

Goodness has its own fire power to pulverize and burn away evil. Thus strong, powerful guitar playing pushes away the forces of evil.

Sor "Etude Number 12": Shoot arrows of goodness across the bridge from inside to outside. Connect two continents with a bridge of goodness.

Create fun, first by having it, then ex-pressing and ex-panding it to the audience. Seize the moment, do it now, immediately. Everything else will take care of itself.

Annette asked me to lead singing at the New Year's party.

Group Song Comedy Show. Plus gaida, then add folk dancing, writing as comedy routines. This could be a whole new show. I can throw in anything, and everything I know and don't know. *The Group song Comedy Show: Anything Goes, and Comes.*

Should I stand for this show? Stand-up comedy. Bring a lousy guitar for the freedom and fun-ny of it. No classical guitar at all. Do I want to make this effort? Only time will tell.)

Thursday, November 2, 2023

Is Group Singing and Comedy my new calling? Or is it a re-treat into sleep, monastery, self, and preparation for the next world? Am I too "tired" to return to public life?

It's a big turning-point question: Will I go forward by adding a group singing show? Or will I go backward, retreat into my fully employed present life?

Do I have the interest, energy, and power to ex-pand again? And am I *really* "fully employed?" Is there room? Is it too much to add a group singing show?

Could classical guitar playing ever be introduced as part of a group singing event? As part of its comedy?

A crack in the ice, a break.

My tremolo is a presentable tremolo now.

Friday, November 3, 2023
November Road

Guitar: Play classical in the middle of Group Song Comedy Show. The scale passage in "Pavane in A" is not "fast" but clear and strong. A pavane is a dance. So is Sor's "Etude Number 12," in 3/4 time. Even "Alhambra" can be a dance. Play it as such.

The goal of "Etude Number 12" is to make Sor soar.

Dance, sway, and roll in my upper body, and even below, in the rocking Sor-Soar Waltz. Dance as I play.

First time "Alhambra" is slow, stately, meditative, sad, a river flowing waltz.

Sor's "Etude Number 12" is merry and soaring, Tarrega's "Alhambra" mystical and deep, with its never-ending question of "Why 2 and 3?" All-is-One is the ultimate truth, and yet Al's accents are on 2 and 3. How wild and strange is that?

The ultimate rebellion against hate and depression is creating fun and joy. So, even though destruction is part of creation—and destruction isn't fun—both belong to the process path.

So take a good walk.

CHAPTER FIVE

Bring Joy to the World

Sunday, November 5, 2023
It's the Bottom Line

Joy, biblical *simcha*, is experience of the Ultimate, the bottom line. In this world of suffering, pain, misery, fear, panic, and noxious challenges, joy is radical, revolutionary, precious, and difficult to find but vital to know.

A good challenge is to find and see this treasured vision in the daily news.

Just Do It!

Amazing how all the great ideas and attitudes I just wrote about have dribbled away. Disappeared! All juice and energy gone.

The cloud of inspiration burst. Sickening chaos, purposelessness, bile-searing emptiness. A black cloud floats overhead. Gloom, doom, vacuity, and depression darken all.

But the wind blows on. . . .

How to dispel the Black Cloud?

When feelings fail, intellect can know what's right. Forget the clouds. Act.

Do it anyway.

Monday, November 6, 2023
Bring JOY to the World

A smile and hello can do it.

It's not complicated. So start there. Folk dance, guitar, song, writing books, all art forms are no more than sophisticated extensions.

Start with a smile.

"Alhambra" joy starts with thumb and finger happiness.

Wednesday, November 8, 2023
Study and Create

"Pavane in C" played at proper tempo is upbeat, exciting, and fun. And this for a mere peacock! (*Pavane* mean "peacock.") It's a highly charged realm of fun.

But how do you get to highly charged?

By breaking the barriers of inertia, lethargy, and indifference. Using will power, force them to fall. "Just do it" is the best way to start.

The Real Pavane

The real *Pavane* begins with a majestic bang! Upbeat, proud, and glorious. Create the historical scene, a rapid light march into halls of fury. The pay-off moment is: Best *Pavane* ever! A heavenly moment. Sor "Etude Number 12," too. Fast, light, colored with whimsy and glory: so much fun! More than that. Almost beyond fun. It's All Together in one Grand Mixing Bowl. A gift. But I worked for it.

Politics: It's nice to see historical waves wash away the dirt. Bullies and idiots don't win forever.

Thursday, November 9, 2023

I know what's right.

Act first. Good feelings will come later.

Paralysis or dive in: It's a choice. Face death by a dive into the stream of life. For panic, take a breath, then use its power to jump. Dive in. Just do it.

Friday, November 10, 2023
Battle Between Good and Evil

Resting in equilibrium. The battle between good and evil is the law of the world. Expect opposition to the good in both myself and others. Always. It is simply realistic.

Hopefully, evil will lose—but not always, and not for long. Hopefully, good will win—but not always, and not for long. In their constant battle, the seesaw never ends.

Accept it as such.

Keep fighting for the good—in me. A few others will follow.

The world is our reflection.

Playing Guitar is About Truth

Seize the tempo of the moment. It's the Truth. Fast, slow, medium tempo depends on flow. Blood speed creates the mood, and the mood of the moment is Truth.

Playing guitar is about the tempo of Truth.

Monday, November 13, 2023
Keep Dancing and Playing!

No tour registrations have come in during the last few days. To my surprise, though, having no business is very peaceful. Can I, should I, get used to this? If I did, I'd be returning to childhood and teenage freedom.

Do I want such freedom? Maybe. Of course, I'd never give up

my miracle schedule with its writing, music, exercise, and study. And folk dance teaching, which to me is really another form of play, would remain part of it.

But what about my tour business? Could I, should I, give it up completely? Or put it at the bottom of my list? Or even better and bigger: Could I, along with money, security, obligations, and responsibilities, make it all part of play? Now that is a real challenge!

How to make my tour business fun, turn it into Playtime Tours. It means turning annoyances, grievances, frustrations, and so-called serious stuff into playful activities. Is there a difference between fun play and serious play? What a tautology. (Polytheism versus monotheism.) Does "serious play" even exist? War games versus real war? Is my tour business a war? Partly. In a cosmic sense, it's all play. Do I have the mental and emotional strength to see the world as a stage, myself an actor, the news events of the day all taking place in a huge playpen? Yes. But it is very hard.

From the point of view of the dead, all is play.

Isn't this also the view of eternal life? Yes. Do death and eternal life go together? Are they the same? Is there really death? Is there really eternal life?

These are great questions that only I can answer with the only thing I have a say in and can control: my attitude. The answers are up to me. Small me, or Great Me.

If all is play, what happens to meaning and purpose?

Wednesday, November 15, 2023
"Just Do It" Breaks through the Illusion of Separation

Drink the juice of discouragement, taste the trembling, teeter-down bitterness of depression. Now see the choice between quitting and just-do-it.

Quitting drives you back in the cycle of the circle. But just-do-it ploughs you into possibility and new territories.

Pavane in C

The audience feels ever present—and it is.

I am never alone. The audience is me, and vice versa. I and Thou transforms into I *is* Thou.

Separation is an illusion.

The black cloud and I have a relationship. We work together. As part of my audience, its black separation is also an illusion. Indeed the black cloud is me. (And truth is, I don't mind a little rain now and then.)

"Just do it" breaks the illusion of separation; it throws me back into the stream of life, Heading downstream, with my audience, we swim together through hot and cold water.

Audience Problem Solved

Strange, I've solved the audience problem. I now have an audience. . .always. I've also solved tempo and speed problems. They all depend on my mood, which the audience will accept, be fascinated by, and even love. Any tempo will work, and is its own adventure, same with any speed.

Performance is also solved.

Any tempo, any style: They all work in their own peculiar way.

Sunday, November 19, 2023

I miss Ma and Pa at our annual Thanksgiving dinner. I'm reading the Torah to remember them and get back some of their stability and protection.

I had a pre-dinner panic attack, frozen in unconscious sadness and horror of the loss of their protections.

But it's better to look ahead. Put the mourning of my former tour-leadership life behind me. Absorb its lessons, but don't look back. Remember Lot's wife. Reject the pillar of salt approach. Embrace positive affirmations.

What's positive about being CEO? It sure *sounds* positive. Ludmila admired and loved it, especially all the growth, new destinations, and directions I've put in. Speaking to her made me re-evaluate myself and replace the November mental vacuum with a new look at CEO Jim Gold International status.

Patience, persistence, judgment, daring, courage to seize the moment, all equal the "just right" of satisfaction.

Do not over-think "just right." Just plunge in and do it.

Muslims pray five times a day; Jews three times a day. I pray with guitar. Music is my morning prayer shawl.

What about practicing/praying three times a day?

Tuesday, November 21, 2023
Protection Racket: Enjoy Suffering, It's All Part of the Plan

After a quick descent into hopelessness, fear, and post-folk dance teaching aches, I once again remembered that even self-knowledge and compassion do not protect me from bad patches. Short dark visits are just part of the plan.

After absorbing and accepting them, go a step further: love them.

And as for depth: Do less and move slowly.

Knowing my frailties connects me to other frail humans.

We're all connected through transience. All we are and do disappears and dies. Couple this with aches and anxieties, and it's quite a mess. Who needs it? Better free and happy. Can't beat the moments of transcendent joy.

It's all part of the pie. A slice tastes good, but the whole pie is our destiny.

Thursday, November 23, 2023

I'm creeping, climbing out of the cleansing trough.

Exercise is the first to appear, with a yoga base.

What will be the yoga beyond the trough, the new yoga? As a start, yoga and Torah are one. Toradic yoga, with knees coming in second. A complete re-examination of body parts. Link lower back to knees to patach, with its glimpse of wisdom.

Guitar: Go deep. Re-connect with the God of Music. Express it light and clear. Heavy on the outside does not mean soft on the inside. But with your foot squarely in the confidence pit, you can "speak softly and carry a big stick." Travel deep within through the black hole to the light beneath and above it. Then drink from the pit of wisdom.

Performing is praying in public.

A story of deliverance. A nice story. The last leaf to fall from the tree. Monkey Joe, disguised in his monk's habit and wearing *tsitsit* around his waist, moves his family from his Flat Bush house Bush Wick to a new home in an upscale neighborhood. Their delivery truck transporting his old furniture gets lost *en route* in the Metaphysical Transportation Center. The old sofas, chairs, bed, wall paintings, and kitchen utensils are never found again.

Family Members

Art, through design, is the center of my tour business. He is a cousin of my idol and inspiration, the God of Music.

Although not the same, they are related.

Writing is part of the family, too.

Remember the connection. After all, I'm a family member, too.

On Boring Others

The statement "You are boring" is a bit different from "Your work is boring". . .but not that much.

It means you're not pleasing others. In the tour business, when someone says my ad or email is boring, it means no sales.

But if my purpose is not to bore myself and not care about sales, what's the difference whether what I do bores others or not? Who cares?

Why should I care? Sure, it's nice to make others happy—even though making them happy is mostly beyond my control.

Certainly, I'd love to have this attitude, a mental place I want and need to be.

Friday, November 24, 2023
Memory

Is memory a legitimate form of vibration? And if yes, does that make memory "real"? In other words, do people and deeds last forever?

How could the answer not be yes? On one level, the vibrational one, nothing ever "dies." It just changes forms. As soon as you remember it, it exists.

This means that eternity exists (along with immortality in the form of spirit), but all on another level.

The memory level.

Memory has, and is, its own phenomenological truth.

But isn't the physical form just a bunch of vibrations? That's why you can re-member the temple, its physical form.

I'm dealing with death and loss here, along with the sadness and fear when it happens. And, on one level, all this will happen.

But how many levels are there?

Importance of my Journal

Is what I write in my *New Leaf Journal* important? Certainly, for me it is. But what about for others?

Ego says I need it to be important for others, too. It reminds me I am important.

But beyond ego. . . ? Well, why not? Believing my journal is important beyond myself is better for me. And better for me is all I can know.

So why not believe the best?

Do I have the strength of imagination to do that?

Dedication

If I dedicate each "Alhambra" note to God and not to man, what happens to the notes? And which aspect of God? The wrathful, joyful, slow-down, focused, fun, playful and lofty? There are many moods and modes of the One God.

In all the above manifestations, God is the focus. Man is not considered; he is left behind, pushed into the background, an afterthough, a glance, a wink, a glimpse.

But man belongs to God. The "Alhambra" notes, as man's representatives in the Congress of the Lord—The Heavenly Congress—represent the spark inside man which belongs to, is part of, God.

So, play for the Nameless Loving Guitar Master, but use all the earthly modes.

Saturday, November 25, 2023
Anti-Semitism

How do I react to anti-Semitism?

Here is the emotional order: shocked, hurt, sad, then a retreat, fear, followed by insulted and angry, and finally propelled to action.

How to fight? Physically, mentally, and spiritually.

What can I do, if anything?

How important to me is my Judaism? Evidently, more than I thought.

Yes I am hurt and angry to my core. What could I do physically? I don't know *karate*, boxing, or other martial arts. So my only resort would be passive resistance: sacrifice my body, be beaten on the street for standing up. Courageous sacrifice like Ghandi's, or Martin Luther King's. Although I would personally love to beat the shit out of these monsters, my only real choice is passive resistance.

My weapons appeal to those with morals and character. Use the weapons I've got. I can shout, "Shame on you!"

Why shame? The battle between good and evil is both internal and external. And in the struggle, they are choosing to stroke, feed, and ignite their evil aspect. They could choose better. But they choose not to. So shame on them!

Only anger, indignation, and love would give me the power and motivation to be hurt, beaten, for my values. (Note how love for my "enemies" gives power to stand up to them.)

Value of My Writing

New Leaf Journal is the adventure of my thoughts and feelings across time and space, how they teach me, and where they lead me.

They may even guide others to write.

The Audience Is Always with Me

The Audience is always with me—around me, listening, watching, and participating on their level, in their own way.

So I need to send out healing vibrations, no matter what. Even after mistakes, pauses, and flaws. All parts of the human condition are on display. Even if boring, if accepted and done by humans, they can be healing.

My job is to think this, and do what I can. If I do, everything else will take care of itself.

Monday, November 27, 2023
Watching the Movie

No Monday morning dread today! What a nice way to wake up.

Then, while I drank coffee, I thought about all the money I'll be spending for dental implants, listened to the morning news, and fears returned in a jiffy.

Does Monday morning dread arise because, on Monday, I face the "real" world? Do I really need it? Is there another way to see things?

It's so obvious: We have no control over results. Only stupid people believe we do, and I am one of them.

We only have control over attitude and effort. (I'm even beginning to wonder about that.)

Maybe anxiety and fears of the future are part of a grand ego trip. Fearing the future gives the illusion I have control over it, that I have some say in my destiny. But fears of the future and its results are also a total illusion. Part of me enjoys this movie, participating in the illusion of reality. But it's nice to know I can always walk out of the theater.

Tuesday, November 28, 2023
Streaming Joy

Is joy painful? Maybe.

Joy breaks boundaries. I cry for its Magnificence as it puts me on the road reaching for the stars.

After a year of questioning, trying to figure it out, I am ready for Phil's YouTube streaming answer. Last night, after dancing, he said I could stream my folk dance class on my YouTube channel. I could also edit the videos I make on my Apple iPhone; the streaming service also offers the option to save the videos. Then I could buy a cheaper, older Apple computer and save and edit them on this Apple product, and thus avoid all the video transfer problems to my PC. Two great ideas.

This is how I could stream folk dance joy to the world.

Streaming released the flood. Barriers down, all open. This *carpe diem* present brings a completion to my post-Covid, going public, always-have-an-audience period.

I could become a public figure again, even a worldwide one, all through YouTube streaming; meaningful and significant, I'd enter and become part of the new world. And stay at home, too!

A winning combination and culmination.

Wednesday, November 29, 2023

The purpose of an obstacle is to waken courage and the fighting heart.

Dissatisfaction is the prelude to creation.

Friday, December 1, 2023

Closet love and passion for intellect: taking it seriously. I read my journal. I liked it, and I maintain confidence in its importance. No one knows better than me whether it's good or not; and there's a thrill to self-contained confidence.

This is coupled to the sudden hope of handling performance anxiety through the power of breathing. Here's how it works. Take my knee, for example: First comes the pain, usually of stiffness; then the fear of the pain and a mental scenario of bad things that will happen in the future due to it. In other words, anxiety. When this happens, I either stop breathing or slow it down to very shallow. Then comes feeling tired, sleepy, achy, whatever.

However, during these events, focusing on breathing changes everything. Anxiety dissipates, and even pain softens (and sometimes disappears). Quite amazing, and so hopeful.

Breathing works for being overwhelmed, too.

And guitar playing: I envisioned playing in Carnegie Hall to an empty, then full, house! Breathing made it easy, possible, and beside the point. Imagine playing at Carnegie with ease. It also works for fears of death.

With the walls of fear and anxiety falling, fun steps in. Milan's

"Pavane" dances; so do I, and of course my audience as well. I send rich, fat bass notes to friends in the balcony.

Saturday, December 2, 2023

God brings certainty, the only certainty.

If limping made Jacob stronger and a better leader, can my knee do the same?

God and Guitar

There is a peaceful certainty in knowing God exists.

This morning, guitar playing is slow and focused. My thumb acts as the Lord's representative, Al Hambra His agent.

So play with certainty.

Wandering on to the Sor "Etude Number 12," I feel my energy leaking.

Thumb—subtle, mysterious, and hidden at the base—pounds rhythmic salvation in musical form.

Sunday, December 3, 2023
Dabbling in Truth

Frustration about how to go live on YouTube fits into the breathing category.

Fear Israel will lose: (breath, and God).

Hope (and belief) Israel will win: (breath, and God).

Breath is pathway to the Divine. Thumb and Al belong to, are part of, the Path. Knee and back, as obstacles, belong to, are also, part of the Path.

A political fear is still a fear. Handle it as such: Breath, God, thumb, audience, knee, and back.

Where I am this morning is totally marvelous! Dwell in its re-membrance. (How long can I last?)

Tuesday, December 5, 2023
Losing Interest in Going Public?

Suppose I lost interest in going public, in fame and recognition. Is this possible, or am I merely discouraged? Or better, am I getting ready to move on to the next stage? Strangely, I see losing interest as a plus, a step toward freedom—losing my ties and attachment to the material world.

I still have the Lord to deal with—that will never go away. But as for the rest. . .study and know monastic life.

All my practice, Covid retreat, aims and goals had the hidden purpose of bringing my art, cleansed and fresh, to the public.

Now that I'm ready and done, I'm not only resisting, I'm losing interest in what was once my grand goal.

The reality is, I'm not pushing my books, or choreographies, either—and I never have! Presently, I only push my tours "out of habit" and to make money, and to practice and learn flyer design.

What I enjoy for its own sake is making art, study, exercise, and a bit of socializing as in folk dance classes. Sales and business have also been part of socializing. All this comes naturally, with-out pushing.

So, do I still need to go public? It's a book-and-concert com-pulsion I feel I "should" do, but that I never follow through on. And it's no fun.

Next stage may well be no interest in going public. Which means no publishing, YouTube videos and streaming, and dreams of someday giving a concert.

Study, create, and exercise instead—the teenage life revisited.

And yes, it's pleasant to make money, especially in the stock market. But the panic is gone.

The fame and fortune disease began after college, when I was trying to figure out what to do in my life. I decided on being a writer because it combined intellect and music. In Music and Art High School I learned I loved music, and in my first year at the University of Rochester, I learned I loved physics, philosophy, languages, reading, literature, study, and learning. Even terrible marks did not dissuade me.

But after graduating from the University of Chicago, when I moved to Greenwich Village to begin my new life, I was a lost soul. No parental support, no identity, no nothing—having to support myself and make it on my own. Scary. So, needing security, I grabbed at fame and fortune. And this although, in my heart, I really was not that interested in it. Maybe I sensed the foundation was based on fear and weakness, not love.

Well, all that was long ago. Now things are different.

Wednesday, December 6, 2023
Liberation Day

The loose, released annularis finger of the "A major Pavane" slips into the "Alhambra" castle, then steps toward liberation of the left knee.

Connect to fun and joy: the purpose of guitar.

Write to Amuse and Explore

I'll never know if my books, or my writing, are good, good enough, or for that matter, even bad. What others say is just their opinion, and theirs is as good as mine. When they say nice things,

I'm happy; and when they don't, I'm not. And that's the end of that. I feel the same about guitar, folk dances, and my books. Aesthetics are all just opinions.

But if that is the case, why bother publishing? In fact, why write? The answer: to amuse and explore. And that's it.

Does writing class help this endeavor? Partly. But ultimately, in this matter, only I can help myself.

Thursday, December 7, 2023
Ride with It

The surface hasn't changed. But I'm moving to the next level of depth.

This morning it was just an old-fashioned depression visiting in a novel "go private" form. What to do? Same as usual. My good things. The cloud will pass.

What have I learned?

Don't pay too much attention to these down periods. Depression and discouragement are passing clouds, black with rain, filled with destruction, but transient, *en route*, passing. Work to survive them. Travel in spite of their misery. My path is good and right. I have to believe in it, stay on it. This is the year of good fruits and fulfillment. That's all I can, should, and will do.

Force myself to write fiction? Would it be good for me? Forcing myself is not "natural." But neither is following my path. (Note: "Just do it" is my mantra.)

Could fiction be part of my Journal?

The serious—beauty and love, and the funny—fantasy fiction, all melted and blended into one Journal.

Establish a deeper relationship with my index finger on guitar. Same pieces, but all different.

Friday, December 8, 2023

With vacant lungs, yearning for air, I drag my windbag self across rock-piled roads pocked with tar pits. And dramatic. I'm leading the wild inner ass to pulmonary gardens, unknown, black-strewn, and strange.

Dare to babble in public.

I've tried making sense of most of my life. Now how about making nonsense? This seems a sensible way to go.

Nonsense may open a whole new world.

Saturday, December 9, 2023
Fruit Fun Road

An energy of love and passion is bubbling up within me. Admit it. Go with it. See where it leads. It's a rededication energy. Well, it's Hanukkah time. Dedication and re-dedication are in order. Harvest is here. Time to gather fun fruits:

Writing: A bubble bath of babbling etymological fruits.

Guitar: Same. Fruit fun plucking from the first touch of the string. "Fruit Fun C Pavane" begins with a pluck-puff. Or is puff-pluck better? The complete "Fruit Fun Pavane Trilogy" follows. (Pavanes compete. Who is the best dancer?)

Folk Dance: Same

Tours: Not yet, but on their way.

Fun is the ultimate rebellion. Fruit fun helps break up the world break up into pieces of laughter, and is thus a high level contributor to the world peace.

You can't have fun without clarity. That's why this dedication is to light, the Festival of Light: Hanukkah. Light as illumination, light as weight, blend and mix as one.

Questions:

Can the mystery of "Alhambra" ("Alhambra" mystery) be fun? (Not yet, but on its way.)

What about the Babble But and Butt etymology twins?

Where is their place in creative writing and literature?

Fulfill the Dream

Now is the time. Transition is over, Covid books are done.

Time to fulfill my dream of earthly fun and heavenly joy. I will start with a one-year commitment: From now on no more roadblocks, no excuses.

Tuesday, December 12, 2023
A Pleasant Bereshit

It's somewhat humiliating to go back to reading *Bereshit* again. On the other hand, reading it is somewhat pleasant.

I also feel like I'm drifting away from the material world. If I am, I can be funny. Drifting brings greater freedom. (A good thing.)

That makes two pleasants this morning.

Think in Hebrew

I won't speak in Hebrew, but I could think in it. What advantage would that be?

Egoless Folk Dance Teaching: The No-Pressure Point

Egoless folk dance teaching: Rather than start the class by taking over, calling for a circle, jumping into it, then leading the dance, I simply play dances my group knows. Then, as soon as they hear the music, they get up by themselves and start dancing, all together in one circle, and without my initiation. I'm not needed. And I dance along with them, not as a leader but as part of the group. I've never done it this way; it's a different experience for me. I feel no pressure to spark, initiate, light the dancing fire, inspire others, push them, start things off. No question it works, and works well. Everyone is dancing and having a good time.

Maybe I'm secretly proud I've reached this point.

Wednesday, December 13, 2023

I'm beginning again, with *Bereshit*, but this time I'm thinking in Hebrew. Why think in Hebrew? To develop a second soul. The second soul needs its own language.

Why do I need a second soul? For the next world. But the next world is here-and-now, today, this moment, the present. If eternity is today, why rush?

Does the joy molecule contain sadness? Probably. But grab it anyway.

Ballad of the Hanging Wrist

"Alhambra" unity and its perfect moment are found in the hanging wrist. All fingers unite. Thus, focus on the hanging wrist.

Hanging wrist is my guitar victory.

Fiction, as seen in the Ballad of Hanging Wrist, is my writing victory.

Sunday, December 17, 2023

Depression and discouragement are agents of rot. They exist always. The battle between rot and substance creation, good and evil, life and death, light and darkness, never ends. Knowing this should be enough to motivate me. I live at the edge of a cliff. Although the sun may shine, I'm still standing at the edge. The dark pit beckons below. I'm aware and afraid: Well, I should be.

Better to be aware. A little fear doesn't hurt either.

Tuesday, December 19, 2023
Classical Guitar Is Not My Calling

Everyone knows and recognizes it but me. Classical guitar is not—and has never been—my gift or my calling. My fiction, folk dance choreographies, songs, and leadership personality are my callings.

Classical guitar playing, really a re-creation of my teenage violin efforts, when I soared happily and freely in my room with its closed door, is my way to relax, float, and dream, my safe vacation escape spot away from the crowd. And I need vacations. . .but vacation spots do not a calling make.

Though over the years, especially as it transformed into classical guitar playing, that departure to vacation, was also a way of hiding from my real gifts and talents. How does one know a calling? It comes easily and naturally. It also takes little to no effort to display it, although to develop it takes practice and lots of work.

Wednesday, December 20, 2023

This is a beautiful and complete freedom charging down, starting with guitar. I played the sweetest "Alhambra," the most relaxed Sor "Etude Number 12," and a lovely "Gavotte en

Rondeau." And this feels like only the beginning.

I wrote this in my journal earlier this morning. I was not going to reveal it, but now I shall.

A New Name

Falling through the pit. The third person "he" still needs a guitar web, and its structure of protection. But change his name to a new person: Larry, Post-Covid Jim, Shoeless Joe Jackson.

On this first day, Larry steps out of guitar-string prison to fly into the sky of freedom, alone, naked, free, and with a new name.

Does he take depression, despair, discouragement, the three Ds, with him? Will they be dropped? Why? Are they still needed for motivation? After all, today is the first day of freedom.

The story begins:

"Saga of Larry Leaf and His Friend Harry Hebrew"

Birth of the Inner Lute. The non-public, unseen, inspiration, invisible fountain of flowing waters, source of guitar within. Hidden behind walls of its secret chamber, a relationship with the Unseen is born, and pearls are created.

This source can never be revealed to a mad public. Impossible. The secret relationship of shining eyes, glint of mischief, source of play, fun and joy. . .indeed, humor and love, are my public talent; meltdown Beauty is my secret. Relationship to the Infinite can only be expressed indirectly through deeds of love, folk dancing, leading, and humor.

Playing "Alhambra" now feels comfortable. Its true meaning for me has been revealed. It allows me to dwell comfortably in

Beauty, the Infinite.

Verbalizing feels strange. Direct expression diminishes Magnificence. Ever a secret. Words cannot express it directly. Perhaps trying to tell others about it is just plain stupid.

But indirection works.

Thursday, December 21, 2023
Bring Joy to the World

In order to do this, bring joy to myself. Once my sun shines, its light will shine on others. How to make the light shine? That is the question.

How did I come to this "bring joy to the world" conclusion? Here is today's journal entry:

Even though I agree and know the old ways of thinking, attitudes) are exhausted and dead, I still feel hurt, angry, and sad. I hate to hear it from others, or even myself. Mainly, I hate the effort I'll have to make to change things, and all for no money or love. No payback. It is worth it? Do I want to bother? Or should I just give the whole thing up?

If I've given up on money and love, what would motivate me to write? Why bother?

But note: I *haven't* given up on fun, on enjoyment! In fact, It's the only reason, motivation, I can find. Yes, I have to make an effort to "achieve" fun, but I do believe in it as an ultimate source of motivation. It is the grand Joy connection.

Aha! So writing has to be connected to, motivated by, fun, joy, the grand Connection. Should I write about this? My story search process has to be fun-ny, humorous, fruitful, joy-ful.

Could joy be a commandment?

Bring joy to the world as the eleventh commandment?

Hey, you. You'd better enjoy it—or else! Force myself to find and do joy. Joseph says, in this week's parsha, "I fear Elohim." You can't beat fear of the Lord as a motivator.

Thus, figure out ways to enjoy knee pain, daily annoyances, and more. *Bring joy to the world:* A daily mitzva challenge!

Some rules and thought patterns: Just because its miserable doesn't mean it can't be fun. Just because it hurts doesn't mean it can't be (fun) joyful.

Friday, December 22, 2023
Salesmanship Is Leadership

Note: Leading does not feel like an effort. Saying, "Let's go and do this!" is easy and natural, so sales are my given "talent" (Greek weight). Easy and natural.

A giant shift: And it took only ten seconds. (But of course, preceded by a lifetime, and a 3–4 year Covid transition period.)

But today, in ten seconds, everything got turned on its head.

If I approach my miracle schedule stuff, and everything else I do, as a salesman, a leader, what new adventures are ahead?

This is a "stop in my tracks" day, a "turn myself in a new direction" day: Salesman/leader. There's no choice, since it has been revealed.

History of Leading

My job, calling, and born with talent is to lead.

It was revealed in first grade when I led the Boys Against the Girls in Barnard School for Girls. Then came conducting the orchestra in Music and Art High School. Then organizing my napkin-folding contest as a busboy at Chaits Hotel, followed a few years later by my social director job there.

Giving concerts must have been another form of leadership. (Although I saw it as "being an artist," it also included the fear factor, since I had to play classical guitar, which had nothing to do with leadership, in fact was a denial of my leadership. I was following, rather than leading, the masters I grew up with, and ever frightened that I couldn't live up to them.)

Folk dancing leading and tour leading came next. No problems there. Again, "easy and natural" leadership positions (but always blunted by my need/desire to prove I could play classical guitar.

Where does writing fit in? I'm not sure. Maybe its so-called "purpose" is that it gives me the quiet, private, personal path I needed and still need for self-discovery. It is a non-public vehicle. (Maybe that's why I have so much trouble selling it.) Same for folk dance choreography. Also a private vehicle. Maybe that's why it's so hard for me to say in public, "I created this dance."

But leading folks, whether in private (no such thing) or in public, is no problem. (Even selling them on what I lead is no problem. My sales attitude, though, is totally awful and wrong since it is one of imposing, forcing, pushing, persuading them to join me. And I totally hate that!)

I'm hoping that changing my attitude from push/shove/impose/force/persuade to leading will change all—inviting them to join this adventure with a "Come on, let's go!" (It's your choice, of course, but how silly not to join me and have so much fun!)

(As a side thing, could I do this on classical guitar? Now that would be a challenge! Experiment. Give it a try.)

First, I have to get them to participate with me. Come on, let's go! With folk dancing or group folk singing, participation is obvious. (And easy for me.) But what about only listening? Solo folk songs, no problem. But "participating by listening" to classical guitar?

Is listening really participation? Or only a subtle form of criticism? Aha, there's the fear. But again, so what? Think about the effort/fear/discomfort motivation syndrome. And use classical guitar as my experiment camp.

Writing As Leading?

Could my writing be a form of leading? I'd like it to be. But that does not make it so. On the other hand, if I have a leadership personality, and if I am a leader, wouldn't that make what I write a form of leadership? I'd like it to be. And logically, it is. (But is it in fact?) If yes, I'd have to sell it. (Salesmanship and leadership.)

Saturday, December 23, 2023
Under the Piñata

Broke the guitar bag piñata. Exercise and folk dance fell out, along with five other marvels. Yes, my body aches, and there are annoyances and death, but it's all part of the game and its new priorities. Under the guitar piñata there are: slow, fast, loud, soft, stiff, strong, tight, loose, sloppy, clear, stunted, flowing, no fun, fun, bumpy, rolling. "Leyenda," "Misionera," "Soleares," "Malats Serenade," all of them, sloppy or fast, who cares? Even songs are free and don't matter.

Monday, December 25, 2023
Christmas Day

I no longer need Hebrew, the bible, or even Judaism to remind me that God is within. I know it without props or reminders.

This means and brings up a new question: Do I still need to read or study Hebrew, bible, or even Judaism?

Maybe continue doing these things I love, but for different reasons.

What reasons? Joy, fun, entertainment, and, in the process, bringing joy to the world. (That, after all, is the name of this *New Leaf*. Certainly, all the pressure to accomplish is gone since the task has been completed.)

Sad, somewhat frightening, but true. The old need for Hebrew, bible, and Judaism have been fulfilled. Or better, my study goals have been internalized. The learning of servant, leader, and salesman have been fused. These old tools have served their purpose. On Christmas day, I am "there" and "here."

Transforming Pain into Pleasure

Note: During guitar warm-ups and playing, no pain. In fact, I never have pain! And if I do, I recognize it immediately and change my method of playing to avoid the pain and change my playing style, attitude, or whatever, and transform pain into pleasure.

Us this guitar approach for exercise and dance. Think, and aim for no pain. Never again! Move beyond stiffness.

Tuesday, December 26, 2023

First tour sale to Western Canada. Excited! Inspired! But what to do? Sell more! Short term goal: Fill this year's tours!

Annoyances

Practice seeing a grain of goodness (light) in every annoyance (darkness}.

Do depression, despair, and discouragement, the three Ds, count as annoyances? Yes.

Wednesday, December 27, 2023

Start *Folk Dance Soul on Fire* bio: *How the Folk Dance Adventure Changed my Life.*

On the Perfect "Alhambra"

It's a skill—so it could last and grow.

What does such a change of clothes look like?

Since it is perfection achieved in life, it is short-lived. What comes after? More perfections—a voyage of dreams and crazy images through an imagined universe. God is watching with a smile.

Writing: I may not have the energy or interest to write my *Folk Dance Soul on Fire* memoir, unless I can make the process humorous and fun.

Also, see the *Wisdom of New Leaf.* Start a *New Leaf: Joy as a Worship Plan.* The grand effort. It means that misery, along with depression, despair, and discouragement, still have their place, a lower landing of tears and humor. But my aim and purpose is to climb Jacob's ladder, to reach and longer dwell in the higher floors of Heavenly High Rise.

Fear still has its place, too. But align it with awe and wonder.

The Magic of Creation

I'm feeling the perennial disappointment and emptiness of meaning when the magic of creating—fresh writing in my *Journal*—passes. So meaningful when I write it; so meaningless when

I re-read it.

In my mind, words have such power when I write them during the fire of creation mode, each syllable alive and sparkling. But once the fire of invention dies, my writing appears old, dried, bland, stiff, innocuous, empty, embers of meaning,

Sunday, December 31, 2023
Pleasant and Uneasy

Reading the Torah in Hebrew: I'm surprised at the ease and flow. But it's still somewhat *uneasy*. Will that ever cease? Slowly over time, I get better. But unease at *something* will always exist. If not, I'll manufacture it as a motivator.

Do I need unease as motivation? Maybe. I like it. But too much is unpleasant. That's where judgement comes in.

Competition

I'm dwelling in broken satisfaction. Running yesterday in the gym on the tread mill, with focus on abs, did it. I broke all my treadmill running records!

Competing with myself, I won! (I hate competing with others, but with myself, yes! Competing with myself is an unease I like! Competing with myself—and winning—brings exhilaration!)

Although yesterday was a good day, today I may lose or forget my gains and drown in unease. So I must dwell in the glory while it lasts. Then comes the crash. But they are only clouds, good and bad, black and white, and all passing. The white cloud of victory is still a cloud, and passing. Yes, I wish it would stay; but hovering and lingering are its limit. Then on to the next.

CHAPTER SIX

Joy as a Worship Plan

Monday, January 1, 2024
Emerging from Sleep

The philosophic turning of a new word or two in my mind, first thing in the morning, is very pleasant, a lovely wake-up brain massage. Not to memorize or remember—although that's okay too—but rather an easy, natural way to emerge from the rest of sleep.

Tuesday, January 2, 2024
Too Easy Is Not That Easy

Is it a New Year's illusion? Due to my attitude change, it seems that things have gotten easier. Is this true, or a temporary lull?

Also, the nimble rat within wants to gnaw at something more, something bigger, to grow fatter and move up the ladder. This rodent is saying too easy is not that easy, even a bit uncomfortable. A Spartan driver is needed to enliven the path, push the inertia-clad soul, raise my goals, expand them. Stop at the wonder point. Dwell in awe for awhile—maybe ten seconds. Then move on to the next, ending with leave-a-room-unfinished (a Bulgarian saying). Dwell comfortably in the incomplete.

Wednesday, January 3, 2024
Connection

Make Hebrew my second language. This starts with loving its sound in my ears, the feel of each word in my mouth, the rhythm of each syllable in my body. This done, I slowly begin to feel it in my gut, and from there it spreads to mind and body.

Do commitment and connection go together? Yes.

Friday, January 5, 2024
Using Enthusiasm and Ecstasy

I need a "little" guitar goal, though.

How about enthusiasm and ecstasy? Do it right away, with no warm-up.

Saturday, January 6, 2024

Historically, go against the Jews and you always lose. In the short run you may win, but long term you fade out, die, and disappear, while the Jews remain.

Confidence

Even though I'm new at this, I'm still coming up with my own translations of Hebrew words in the Torah. Maybe I'm really not so new. After all, I've been in this linguistic stuff for many years, twenty, thirty, I'm not even sure. By now I'm a veteran. So it's reasonable that I have my own views about translations and the "real" meaning of words.

That's why I don't really need a teacher. It's nice to discuss these things with knowledgeable people, and I'll listen if I hear something new and interesting. But mostly, it's just to confirm what I already think. This means I either have *chutzpah*, *hubris*, or confidence.

I've been through many years of *chutzpah* and *hubris*, which are really a lack of confidence in disguise. Now I'm leaning strongly toward confidence.

I heard someone on the radio say her New Year's vow was to give up fear. I like that. So I'm vowing to give up fear for a year. Try it. See what happens.

Start with fear of being overwhelmed by all the things I think I must do, then move on to fear of body aches (but to real pain, I'll continue to listen).

Flaming Finger Tips

Guitar: Focus on the flaming soul of each hungry fingertip sparked by enthusiasm, burning with ecstasy, flowing upward.

I Love My Folk Tour Business!

Heavy lately, something is lodged deep in my bones. What it is, I'm not sure. Then I read an article about Buddha and Moses, how they both started out in the palace, then went outside and saw the real world of suffering, left their palaces, and became religious leaders. Suddenly, I broke down in tears. Why? I'm not sad. Actually, things are going pretty well. Then I realized I'm crying for happiness! I broke down for the Magnificence, the magnificence of the Covid period and restructuring of my lifestyle, attitudes, soul and body, and am still feeling the permanent after-effects of that transformation. I'm crying because I'm happy to return, to come back into business, to start selling and promoting my folk dance tours, happy to be back, but this time as a free man!

Somehow I'm loving what I'm doing—my ads and email designs, sales, even calling folks. Somehow my business, which used to be a pressure, strain, annoyance, and worse, has become a joy! Nothing has changed, yet everything has changed. Happy to be a businessman, entrepreneur, salesman, president and CEO of my company. Hard to believe or imagine, but it's now a joy! I'm crying with laugher, and laughing through the tears. This is the first time ever in my life that I can say I wholeheartedly love entrepreneurship.

Tuesday, January 9, 2024
Aiming for the Five E's: Healing the Self and World One
Enthusiasm at a Time

Maybe I shouldn't give up my kind of "fear" so quickly. Maybe it's good for me.

What is my kind of fear? And what makes it different? It's productive. Although I call it "fear," others might call it excitement, even inspiration. So far, I've not been able to reposition and name it in such positive words. They just haven't worked for me. But perhaps now, I might want to learn how to use them.

Indeed, a good challenge: When I get a good idea and decide to act on it, do it. How can I rename the nervous churning that stings my stomach, wrenches my gut? Call it excitement? In the past, my "belief" in fear, and the combo of depression, despair, and discouragement energized and motivated me. Do I still need them?

Wednesday, January 10, 2024
The Power of "Alhambra"

The power of "Alhambra" as healer offers a different vision and purpose for classical guitar. Heal the sick. Pour notes into the nursing home, release the numb and semi-dead, wake them gently from stupor, quiet and calm fears and anxieties.

Conceive of dance steps the way. Yes. In truth, they are the same. I only have to think it.

Thursday, January 11, 2024

If panic is extreme fear, and some interpret fear as "excitement," perhaps underneath most panics are excitements. This would mean that panic is suppressed excitement.

Here's a good thought: Since I vowed not to fear anymore, why not expand the process to include panic? View panic as an extreme version and suppression of it.

Sure, I'm vulnerable. But I'm also smarter. Having lived on the fumes of old habits for the past few weeks, I smell the fumes fading, blowing away.

Let's look at inability to get more customers for my tours. An embarrassment. I'm letting my travel agents and suppliers down. I can choose to make the maximum sales effort, but results are up to the Higher Powers. So on the positive side, failure makes me humble.

Although I like thinking I'm independent and don't need approval, truth is, pleasing others is what I want and maybe even need. I love pleasing others when I can; and I'm so disappointed when I don't. No wonder I'm nervous before a show, a performance. A performance is about pleasing others. Otherwise, why bother?

Maybe that's why Buddhists, and so many other philosophers and religions, say life is suffering. I mostly agree. (Well, if you can't give up suffering at least you can suffer on a higher level.)

When I perform at anything, teaching folk dancing, running a tour, giving a guitar lesson, whatever, my job and goal is to please my audience.

What about pandering? Pleasing means doing it on my terms, with my values. Pandering is the opposite.

Posthumous Tours: A Future-Looking Memoir

In the distant future, which is now, how will my Jim Gold International dance groups travel? What countries will we visit? How will Hungary look in the future?

They say that, to know the future, understand the past. As a

start, I could look at my past tours to Hungary, former Czecho-
slovakia, and in fact, all the tours to the twenty-seven countries
that I've organized and led. This could be my guide to future
travel.

In fact, what the *csikos* (horsemen) of the *puszta* and Horto-
bagy Plain wore when they rode in a wild circle around us in 1984
might give me a clue to their dress codes for our August 2180 tour,
or even the July trip of 3002.

More questions: In 3196, will it be too hot to travel during the
summer? Or too cold? It is an unknown fact that in his first epistle
to Saint Stephen (Szent Istvan), founder of the first Hungarian
state, the 19th-century Hungarian poet and sage Arany Janos
asked, "In a thousand years, will the earth still exist?" (The King
answered in Latin: "Quid mihi prodest quod maiorem sapientiae
dedi operam?" or "Does it really matter?")

Friday, January 12, 2024
Turning the Five E's into Six

If I don't have the pressure to be macho and fast, what's left?
Only Enthusiasm, Excitement, Effort, Energy, and Ecstasy. Now
I'm adding a sixth: Enjoyment.

Am I sad about losing, giving up, depression, despair, and discouragement? Partly. A bit of mourning over losses is natural and
in order.

Guitar: Finger Flush

A finger flush, quantum physics riot, red, strong, and fun. Elec-
trons moving wild and free in any direction. Doesn't matter. Anything can happen. A daring dive into the (tremolo) joy pit: wild

and swirling, fingers dancing until they drop. That's the exhaustion point. It stops—but you don't die. Rather, you move on. . .to the next finger flush.

Saturday, January 13, 2024

The bridge of Torah study. . .to somewhere else.

I'm ready for a different linguistic commitment. The Hebrew model cracked, and the Torah bucket broke. What will spill out? Shock, and quick sadness/mourning over the rupture.

But after the surprise ending of my six-month Torah-study route, I'm circling back to a creative vacuum and a clearing of the path for a deeper linguistic connection, to tours and talking to people. (Amazed I just said that.)

Add Bulgarian, Greek, and Spanish.

Spanish connects to the gym, Peru, and Martha and John Tavera; Bulgarian to gaida (Ventsi Andronov and Niki Enchev) and Ventsi Milev; Greek to Maroula Konti and Lee Otterholt; Hebrew to Joe, Jim Freedman, and Jim and Etty Schwartz.

I sensed I needed some God in me. So I took the six-month Torah detour.

Did I get what I needed? Maybe. I hesitate with yes. Too strong, fixed, and definite. God is fluid. Quantum physics implies it.

Loving Languages

I love languages.

It's thrilling to learn a new word, and (hopefully) someday soon, master and use it.

Learning a new skill is so elevating, inspiring, and joyful.

Sunday, January 14, 2024
Dealing with Discomfort by Living at the Edge

The fear that I can't, shouldn't, or won't give up is called "awe." Awe—as found in "awesome," is experiencing chills, trembling, and fear of Majesty and its powers. It's the fear you never want to lose or give up.

Awe displays itself, arises, shows up, at the edge. That's why living life at the edge is awesome. But it's also uncomfortable.

How to deal with discomfort? Learn the art of living at the edge. Practice makes better. And I like perfection too, even thought it only lasts seconds.

How to practice awe? Give up control. How do I practice giving up control? By just doing it!

Control and Giving Up Control

I practiced giving up control on guitar. By the fifth practice session, it worked. How to control my lack of control? How to control giving up control? Asking the question is another form of control.

So don't ask. Just do it.

Monday, January 15, 2024
Cripple Power: Wise-Fear/Smart-Fear

Thrills and chills of happiness/sadness. Give up control. A partnership. Unified. A good thing.

Fear blends into excitement, and vice versa. Imagine their unification, the very definition of excitement, the milk and honey of discovery.

Lymphedema, left leg, and being crippled also follow this pattern and this Covid cleansing path. They represent the poisons of strength; in my mind and body, they have hidden power.

Poisons are transformed into privilege and progress, mental twists into physical ones, and ideas become material creations.

Hidden power? Do I dare think such a thing? Where is the proof?

Wild ideas, losing or rather giving up control: All good stuff. Cripple power equals triple power, and it is rising.

My existential fear of running wild has lost its grip. The child-soul has passed through the gates. Now I am. And its no longer hard, a big deal. In fact, it feels easy, a done deal. "Alhambra Fat Leg," not a happy name but a happy thought. A fresh symbol of tolerance and joy has come to life.

Tuesday, January 16, 2024
Performing in the Whirlwind

The inner whirlwind matches the outer one. Start with the former, then connect. Lose control. Dive in. Audience and whirlwind are soon one. Not a big deal.

Grandchildren and great-grandchildren are a great audience to practice on. A first. The city enters our home. What shall I pour into them? Start with beautiful, pure notes.

Dr. Guitar Appears! Crushing Boundaries with a Single Pluck

Playing guitar for Violet and Etty. At a distance, healing and soothing. Etty's leg operation anxiety diminishes as resonant, uplifting chords, power plucked single notes, drift her way—vibrations waving away pain while warming blood and bones.

Calm the mind, sooth the soul, here or at a distance: a new kind of concert.

I can do it. This is a concert I can give every day, make it part of my life, and I don't even have to leave the house! I've always wanted to give a concert. Maybe this is the kind I've always wanted to give.

Wednesday, January 17, 2024

Give imaginary concerts. Cuts down on travel and audience pressure.

Flowing

It starts with six-month old Violet and family, then moves to (healing) Etty.

The infant is a bit tougher today. Not just a lump. She has blended (almost disappearing) into a blaze of glory. Tough, hard, digging in, strong, and good. Flowing!

My Fear Is a Good Thing

Locked in house for two weeks. Life interrupted. What to do? How will I imagine and handle this challenge?

Keep my rituals—in front of others! The performance continues. It is all good, but now in public. Save myself first, but in doing so, I save others by showing, demonstrating a courageous lifestyle. So, bottom line, I need courage to do what I know is right.

On the Importance of Memorizing a Word

Memorizing a new Hebrew word, hanging on to it like a life raft, gives me a sense of security but also accomplishment. Both are very important.

Do security and accomplishment go together? Evidently. My challenges are accompanied by a fear that I will not accomplish my task, that my enemies and friends will overwhelm and suffocate me.

I now know that this wild, bone-chilling, threatening fear, although hard, difficult, annoying, a pain in the ass, is a good thing. Its challenge alerts and wakes me up! It's a real threat. Why is this imagined threat real? Because if I don't fight against and deal with it, I will be defeated, depressed, and feel worthless, like dying.

Alhambra Life Style: (On the Nature of Aches and Pains)

The aches in my guitar-playing shoulders, these tight muscles creating havoc in my arms, are fear in my bones. They appear in closed energy packets, locked in boxes of energy. My job is to unlock them. I feel pain and the fear of pain. The latter is the locked energy portion, God's way of transferring energy through the soul to the body. The clearer the soul, the freer the flow. This would mean a totally relaxed, un-pushy lifestyle based on natural flow.

Friday, January 19, 2024
Loving My "Alhambra"

This is uniting self-love with Self-Love.

I have to love my own "Alhambra" notes. Period.

The thoughts and opinions of others, although interesting, don't matter. It's up to me. I am my own leader. They will follow, or they won't.

Loving and accepting each note of my "Alhambra" is in my court. Sure I want love from them. And, of course, I already get it most of the time. But it really doesn't matter how much I get if

I can't accept it. It's up to me to love and do so.

Where am I in this adventure into self and universality?

Here's what's happening: The family—Zack, Zane, and Maida—arrived yesterday bringing baby Violet, making us the grandest of grandparents.

Hebrew: a shift toward speaking, and in guitar, toward the public and "performance." Speaking, performance, family. I've "lost" my private self. I'm feeling nauseous as I'm dragged, pulled, drawn into the public on a visceral level.

Seems like it's about control. I no longer control my destiny, having given it to the audience. (Or have I merely given it *up?*) What about sharing? Both are better. But the big Both (as in All-is-One) is best!

Competition and rivalry belong in the world of opposites—opposition as helper, enemy as friend, rival as growth partner.

I'm seeing a new start with all of us together, in public.

Do I dare reveal myself in this manner, vulnerable and raw? But I'm also tough and resilient, if rejected.

"If." That is the new word. Maybe I will be accepted and loved. And this in public! But it has to be done by the deepest, inner me. I'm the one who needs this new, fresh, infant imagination and vision. I'm the one. Others may follow or not.

I have to love the notes. There's nothing left but that.

Once I do, I can love the public.

Saturday, January 20, 2024
Land of Performance

Torah study has lost its energy. I'm blank now, a touch of emptiness and panic. I'm ready for the next stage. But what is it?

Loving my "Alhambra" notes means loving my audience. Performing? Scary. Dropping the Torah/Hebrew curtain. Protection gone. I would be naked and vulnerable performing before the audience. But God is now protecting me.

I have created a great imaginary voyage in my mind. Part of it is the "Alhambra" illusion problem. Why did I create it? At this point, who knows—or cares?

The demon of self-hatred and self-loathing goes so deep. It takes years, sometimes even longer, to nab the bummer and destroy it. Performance is the next step. I may never actually perform, but at least I will be able to.

Not much may change but my attitude—which means everything changes. Since I am different, the meaning of performing becomes different. Coupled with love, it can equal enjoyment.

Sunday, January 21, 2024
The Violet Saga in Three Pavanes: Pavane in C (Let's See and Let's C Pavane)

First Round: Entrance (birth).
Hesitant steps, then more confidence
Triumphal march
Finale: I am here!
Pavane in A
Second Round:
Young adult: Questions and complications, fog in the city, unclear but hopeful.
Pavane in D
Third Round:
Contemplative, thoughtful attitude. Life can be tough, confusing, lots of problems, but beneath/above it all, upbeat prevails. All okay. (Compared to death, life is a bargain).

All three Pavanes are in Major keys (despite Minor key events). Live in a Major key mode. It's better that way.

As for "Alhambra" travels: Keep your eye on the clarity prize. (A lower vision focus splatters mud on the window.)

Side thoughts:
Some aches, pains, even numbness, can be distractions from clarity. The question is always, which ones?

"Alhambra" Alert

The Wake-Up "Alhambra" starts on the first note: a thunderous, definite, vibrating A announcement, sending chills of peace, security, and goodness through the universe. Big Thumb and its following are here, smashing our way forward, spreading joy, love, and unity among our denizens, along with some kick-ass, earthly, aggressive, in the weeds, wow, and knock-'em-dead attitudes.

Wednesday, January 24, 2024
Audience Victory

Audience victory. That is a new term. It starts with stock market trading victories feel so wonderful! From there it moves to guitar victories: trading in thumb-dumb me for thumb-dominant audience victory.

Practice the Art of Organic Joy

Organic joy is a skill, a deep and difficult practice. Thus, to learn and get better at it requires daily practice.

The practice, the skill, the art of en-joy starts with a thought: Think the joy idea. Then move it deep into the bones, muscles, blood, see the veins filled with its hot-blood contents, feeding joy nutrients to every cell as it flows through your body. Then let it expand, spread out. . . .

Tuesday, January 30, 2024
Al's Bass is Easy

Guitar warm-up: At end, a fast, and very fast scale. Speed practice. Folk dance and exercise warm-up, too. End with a quick speed practice.

Once accepted, Al's bass is easy.

Guitar

I'm grateful and happy for my index finger and its "maher" connection. I have two powerful fingers: index and thumb. But thumb is the master and in charge, always. Index can be the first commander.

Clear and Strong

Nothing lasts forever—nor should it. I have and own great memories.

Time to appreciate them and move on. To what? A stabilized existence. My stuff is in order. Okay, so now where's the challenge? None, yet. February is "stable" month. Dive in. Get used to it.

But stable is kind of boring. Although my stuff is in place, it's probably only for a day or so.

I remember concert performances and leading tours. These great moments are gone and over. Guitar playing is also in the memory cycle. I have absolutely no thought of ever performing, giving concerts, again. Just me playing for God. (Not a bad audience.)

Maybe what I really mean in words like "performance" and "concert" is never to use them again. I need a new term, word, or phrase.

Of course, all my old fears (of performing and giving concerts, even leading tours, knees, and pre-performance anxiety) are now only memories, too.

Radical Guitar

This could be my radical guitar way: Play Sor "Etude Number 12" real slow. Wring and drip out the notes, one by one and cluster by cluster. Slow, thoughtful, philosophical, beautiful, my way.

No one listening, or they are all listening.

Both okay.

And if I happen to try a fast one, that's okay, too. Depends on the mood. Let mood rule (not the audience, or preconceived notions.)

TMS Move On

The better I play "Alhambra," the worse my legs and knees get. And my lower back acts up to the point where I feel almost crippled and can hardly walk, never mind go up or down stairs.

Interesting, fascinating, a bit scary, too. The ten-day visit, plus the Al mop-up, has left me in a wake of rage. Add the frustrations of learning HubSpot and setting up the Stride payment program, and *voilá*, TMS moves from "Alhambra" into my legs, knees, and lower back.

Monday, February 5, 2024
A Whole New Way of Playing Guitar: The Slow, Thoughtful
Way

Stumble along. Baby steps forward.

The inner child rises.

Is the fear of being disabled, not functioning, worse than the fear of death? And what about the humiliation? With disability comes humiliation. Is humiliation worse than the fear of being disabled? Humiliation, what others think of me, is a bottom-line fear. In other words, what the audience thinks is a big worry.

The root of humiliation is Latin *humus*, "soil" or "earth." Humiliation never feels "earthy," but I do feel soiled.

In any case, it all started with the grandchildren visit. As usual, I put on my wise grandfather act. When they come, I voluntarily give up my child self. But when I do, secretly, even unconsciously, I'm angry about losing, giving up, that beloved self. Better would be to proudly display it as a truly wise (and courageous) father or grandfather would.

The inner child has to be fed. Displayed, too. Otherwise, I cheat myself and others by giving only half of me. The child self is also not worried about humiliation. And neither is the really wise and courageous adult. Truth is, both are where I want to be, and who I am.

So what's the big deal? Just present both of me and be done with it. I am, after all, a both kind of guy.

Realizing this, move on to guitar.

I opened, warmed-up, as usual with my left-hand legato exercise. Adding my second finger for the first time symbolizes a new child start, a step away from my teacher, Alexander Bellow. I don't need to rebel, but rebellion is the first step.

How can I bring the playful child back into my classical guitar playing? *Back?* She was never there in the first place. "Classical" always meant playing the way the so-called "adults" played. No playful child presence at all. Well, thankfully, those days are gone!

Play fast one-fret guitar scale lightly and playfully.

Light and playful are childlike playing. Add them everywhere.

A whole new my way of guitar playing: the slow, thoughtful way!

Tuesday, February 6, 2024

My folk dance class will cure me. . .or else! Same with guitar. Cure equals inspire. Building a new guitar foundation: fast, light, and right. There's also slow, long, and deep. . .but not for today.

I'm feeling discouraged by my challenges. But note: This down comes after my Stability Victory. So an old pattern returns but with new excuses. Truth is, I've had lots of victories recently. I'm living in Victoryville. No wonder I'm down. Winning, like losing, is a by-product of the struggle, a blip along the way. They're even discouraging and depressing if I focus on them too long. Best to say hello, then follow it with a quick goodbye.

I need new challenges. I thrive on the glory of the struggle.

Wednesday, February 7, 2024

Evidently, I always want to try to get better. The effort, the attempt, is what is most important. I have rest stops along the way. But as I rest, I can still think about improvement, trying to get better.

I'm happiest on this road.

Today it is guitar. Equality between thumb and fingers. Equality (but not equity).

Running

My post-Covid link to happiness is running and the runner's high. How I have missed them. Time to return.

Always Something Not Working

Computer, body, business—there is always something not working. Very frustrating. But a fact of life.

How does anybody get used to it?

Thursday, February 8, 2024
Glory Versus Disgust

Does the sickening feeling I did too much, I ruined it, make any difference? How about choosing to feel glorious and proud for trying so hard? Not the subject, but the attempt: It is the effort of trying to achieve that makes it glorious. The greater the effort, the greater the glory.

Results are hard to interpret. Only you can decide whether they are good or not. But no matter what they are, it is effort that brings Magnificence and glory. Lack of success is not the same as failure. Failure is when you give up. (Although giving up negative roads can be good thing. In this case, paradoxically, failure is a success.) But for me it is to find a worthy venture, then give it all I've got.

Friday, February 9, 2024
Explosive

A whole new way of learning online: Start with HubSpot tutorials.

Do love of learning and security go together? Yes. Learn to be secure, deal with fear, take care of yourself.

Maybe I'm appreciating the beauty of HubSpot, tech, organization, the guitar, and explosive power because, somehow, the internal pressure has been lifted.

Somehow years of inner goals and demands have fallen off, drifted away. (At least for this morning. Note this immediate diminishment of my accomplishment! Very nice. Back to appreciation.)

This is a fresh visit of inner freedom. Even the three-finger web of three-note clusters in Sor's "Etude Number 12" is loosening, falling apart, and through its former tight joints flows a feeling of warmth, focus, love, and beauty. Now each finger gives from its proper place.

The secret poetry of guitar playing: I'm its fortunate practitioner. Is that one reason why I have been given the ability, and desire, to write? To reveal the secrets of guitar and music?

Is there a higher purpose to these skills? I'd like to believe so. (Touch of hubris, humility, diminishment here? Or the truth?)

Sunday, February 11, 2024
The No Pressure Self-Improvement Road

I'd like to think that, through my ups and downs, I am constantly improving.

Well, if I I'd like to think that, why not act so? Who's stopping me? No one except, of course, me. I am choosing my road, which really means I am choosing my attitude.

Since I love to improve, why not stay on my self-improvement road forever?

What stopped me in the past was the belief that the self-improvement road had a final goal, and that, once I reached it, its purpose ended. I had arrived, and there was no place else to go, and thus no reason to stay on the self-improvement road. So, in the past, every time I accomplished something, after the immediate high, I would get depressed and lose my motivation, purpose, and reason for existence. How depressing.

But now, I'm thinking differently. Here's how:

Although I began this morning feeling empty and burned out after diving into my usual morning bit of Hebrew study, I picked up my guitar. I always begin with warm-ups, legato, scales, arpeggios. Sometimes I even warm up with a slow piece. This time however, I realized, as I played my "Pavane in C" opener, that I was giving up the term "warm-up" and exchanging it for "opener." Somehow, beginning with "Pavane in C" was no longer a warm-up but an opener. This change in language felt very important to me, but I didn't exactly know why. Now I'm thinking it signals an attitudinal change.

What kind of change? It feels like an improvement.

Suddenly, I heard *quietly and easily explode* in my mind. That's how to play my "Pavane in C" opener. And I did. Then went immediately to "Alhambra." To my happy surprise, for the first time, I gave up the treble completely.

I knew I was making progress. And I love it. And I realized, knew, that on a cosmic level, although there was no place to go (since I am already there), on a personal earthly, guitar level, I am making progress.

And it's not depressing because, even though I am already there (always, since All-is-One), on my personal (earthly) path, I have an endless way to go. And on this fresh No Pressure Self-Improvement Road, I can endlessly improve.

Yes, it's a paradox—I can improve endlessly, and yet there is no further place to go. This means there's no pressure. I can stay on this path forever.

My eyes blur as I write. This used to be the prelude to a headache. But though my vision is blurry, there is no headache.

Am I secretly angry at something? Maybe. Could it be that my battle is over and won? That I no longer have to fight against myself, that I can accept my love of self-improvement? Am I losing my old arguments and feeling good about the way things are going?

I sense it is the latter. I'm not used to this level of acceptance.

Birth pangs. Blurring but without pain. Babies' first vision is a blur. But as the days go by, blurred vision turns into clarity.

Good Pain Versus Bad Pain

I have lots of pains. But I must admit that most of them are good pains: stiffness, lack of warm-ups and blood flow, aches of unused joints and muscles. Once they're in use, the pains disappear.

Which means these pains are warm-up ones, the good ones. Bad pains come from actual injuries. When I feel them, and, with exercise, they get worse, then I know it's time to pull back, stop, and rest. The good pains lubricate my joints and muscles with healing, oxygen-carrying blood. All good.

Learn to welcome good pains, see them as health-creating gifts, wake-up calls to enliven life and body. Sometimes, it is true, fear accompanies pain.

Are there good fears and bad ones? Yes. A good fear is like jumping off a cliff. A bad fear is stiffness pain that translates into anxieties about self-injury, crippling, disability, and other forms of self-destruction, which discourage you from exercising.

Pain and fear are often companions. But they don't have to be, if I can distinguish between the good and bad. And I can: Years of dancing, exercise, training, experience, and self-knowledge have taught me to know the difference.

Getting Used to the Sunny Room

I may be angry at losing, giving up, my long-held reasons for depression. I may partly resent it; after all, depressions are restful. On the positive side, they're an excuse to take a break from pressures of work, self-improvement, even life itself.

Resistance to success and its feelings does not die easily. I've taken my first baby steps through the door into a strange, richly furnished room with lots of sunlight. Perhaps it's the power of this light that give me a "blinding" headache. I am now living in this sparkling, sunny place. Getting used to it will take time.

Monday, February 12, 2024
Re-Invention

I miss doing things in this world (lead a tour, teach a folk dance class, give a concert, do a reading, run outside: mostly work stuff). Wistful. But I've done it all. Should I do it again? I miss involvement in the physical world. Social life is okay but has no grit. Business, with its annoying highs and lows, has grit. I like grit.

How would going back look? Not really a re-turn but a forward movement.

Life, Imagination, and the Dream

The dream is what I'm after. Life is in the imagination. So is motivation. Reinventing myself is also in my imagination. Which means it may never physically happen, or it may, but either one is okay. The motivation is what I'm after. Actual physical events themselves may just be too annoying to do again. The pressure is off.

But dreaming about them is beautiful and so much fun.

Tuesday, February 13, 2024
Attitude of Commitment

I have no control over winds of change. But I do have control of my attitude toward the wind. My attitude chose commitment to trading because I love the exciting ups and downs of the ride.

Today the market sank 700 points. I lost. But win or lose, I made the commitment.

I hate losing; I love winning. But long term, so what? Win/lose is the nature of the game. Stop complaining, dig in, re-seize the commitment, and move on.

Wednesday, February 14, 2024
Exploding without Injury

Neanderthal Jim has walked away.

But don't discard him. He should be remembered as an important historical item, a relic of ancient times similar to our Paleolithic ancestors, surviving on wits, muscle, guile, and brains. But with fire, the wheel, the computer, and cell phones dramatically transforming everything, survival is different.

Neanderthal Jim needed to change and did, starting with his hands. Today, his thumb thinks differently. So does his old lyre-playing friend Al. Their ancient, pre-thumb finger-power attitude, which shielded them from contemporary life, is no longer useful. Now they proclaim the wisdom of Thumb Power, with its focus on ele-mental, funda-mental, mental, as well as spiritual events.

Speleological explorations went with him. Post-cave stuff has arrived to help him move out of his cave. Techniques and inventions to free the faithful inner poet, engine of his soul, have moved in. Powers beyond the dark underground, explosions without injury from wild animals, have been released.

Explosive power dispels fear and creates immediate focus. Neanderthal Jim now runs daily and dances with strong feet and good knees. He holds the Constitution of Market Ups and Downs acceptance certificate high in his right hand.

The Poet Explodes

The poet explodes.
So does the artist,
Businessman, entrepreneur,
The linguist, historian, athlete, and trader.
Began today
To speak and hear Hebrew
And the Pavane explodes in C.

Thursday, February 15, 2024

Disturbed my mind with obligation: to write about guitar. Of course, no one is obliging, pushing, forcing me to write but me.

This puts guitar on a different level: no longer a performing tool, but a writing tool, a tool of self-expression.

I gave up performing on guitar. If I give up tours and my tours business, or even folk dancing, would I want to write about them? Does giving up the actual doing of things create more space in the imagination, and, as such, expand the creative mind, and in my case, get me to write about them?

An idea is taking over my brain, forcing me to write. It is disturbing. I don't want it. I'd prefer inner peace. But it feels like this is happening almost beyond my will.

The obligation enters from Out There and finds room to grow in my mind. Is such an explosion of potential a calling?

Truth is, on a cosmic level, everything is connected. There is no outside and inside. Both already exist in me, but only as potential. I can choose to actualize them or not—one way or the other, the potential exists. That's nice to know. (Am I creating a grand rationalization for avoiding all this effort? Probably. Wait and see.)

Friday, February 16, 2024
Explosive Approach

The "Alhambra" theme is in the bass. Thus right thumb leads to the bottom-line truth.

Do I regret all those years of treble going in the wrong direction? I was fighting for my life. The need for survival forced me to avoid facing the truth of Thumb.

Can I forgive myself? Do I regret "wasting" all those (guitar-playing) years? But I couldn't have done it any other way. I had to control, even deny, my power in order to earn a living, to survive.

What was my fear during those years? That I would give in to this inner power, explode, go in all directions, lose my business, hurt myself and my family. I had the power all along but held back; I wouldn't give in and release it, to protect myself and family.

A pleasant thought or excuse. But those days are over. I'm at the doorway of thumb power. I'll learn from my regret by vowing never to give up or deny this power again.

How will that work?

My physical power has diminished. (This seems like a normal

aging progression.) But mental and spiritual power have grown. How will that affect my life?

Saturday, February 17, 2024
Book of Guitar

I've been on the right-hand guitar road for years, trying to straighten out my emotional and spiritual life. Now evidently, it is in order, so I can focus on the gross left-hand road of material and physical guitar-playing reality.

So I began the morning by asking this guitar question: "Do I have the confidence to focus on my left hand, the gross, material aspect, versus my right hand, the emotional and spiritual? Yes. My emotional and spiritual lives are in order and can take are of themselves. I am to start out on the left-hand road. And its question is: How lightly can my left-hand fingers press the strings and fingerboard, and survive? Too lightly, the sound is a thud, muffled. Too hard, and wasted energy affects my emotional and spiritual guitar-musical life.

Living in Paradox

I'm reading about the hidden messages in water. Should this begin my study of Japan and Korea, too? Is it too much? Will I fall apart, become unfocused? Or will I explode, meaning, like water, expand in too many directions? Is this an avoidance of narrow focus, á la guitar? Or an expansion of focus to include the whole universe?

I sense it is the latter, expanding when I "should be" contracting, broadening when I "should be" narrowing. Paradoxically, this is a cautious explosion. So I'm living in paradox. Or perhaps this fearful phase of my life has ended. Time to cautiously explode, dive in, expand in all directions. All-is-One is, paradoxically, the broad definition of a narrow focus.

Is all this just another morning fantasy? Am I simply having fun with my imagination through writing? Maybe. But that's okay, too. And you never know where it may lead.

Sunday, February 18, 2024
Self-Expression

Tell my story even though, or if, it is miserable and funny.

Self-expression: Moving easily from guitar to writing since both are forms of story-telling. Inspiration and explosion mean the same thing, only the former is an artistic, poetic word, the latter more for physical, athletic events.

At this late, advanced stage, I can mostly forget about technique and focus on the true purpose of art in general, and guitar playing in particular—namely, self-expression.

Monday, February 19, 2024
All "Alhambras" Are Good—For Something

Since life is flow, every moment is different, and how I feel at any moment is different, so every "Pavane" I play expresses something different. I play the "Now Pavane" filled with truth, because that's all there is. I give the audience every guitar note. I hand (and finger) it over to them. Will they accept this gift? Not up to me. I can only offer. That is my function, my job. I have control over job attitude but not results.

Of course, on a cosmic level, all notes reach the audience. Part of my job is remembering this transcendental fact. If I do, I can subtly, quietly, even secretly transmit it to them, and thus remind them of their transcendence. Divisions, separations, and differences, although interesting, are an illusion. Actual and potential exist forever. Slow has fast within it, and vice versa.

The slow "Alhambra" has its own truth. So does the fast one. They just sound different. No matter the pace, all "Alhambras" are good for something.

Tuesday, February 20, 2024
Fearless Money Flow: The Beauty of Money

How to receive tour deposits and full-payment money with credit cards in my website? Stripe login and WordPress gravity forms—I don't understand them.

And I run away from this annoyance. Does this payment fucker ever work right? And how does it work? How to integrate Stripe into my WordPress website?

What will motivate me to learn about Stripe, Ecommerce, or WordPress gravity forms?

The next stage: Crack the money code. Find beauty in forms, understanding, and money. (And connect them to guitar.)

Such capitalist thoughts about the blood of business used to make me sick, nauseous: They generated fear, lowliness, crawling in the mud of trepidation, bad, wrong, evil. But I also need money, and truth is, when deposits and full-tour payment checks arrive in my mailbox, as I always say, I see them as a form of love.

Yes, I have been conflicted about money most of my life. I like the power, protection, and security it gives me. But I also like the artist's life of adventure, insecurity, and hanging over the abyss. A conflict. Of course, you need both, a balance. A calm, balanced walk is one between the extremes.

But who needs or wants that? Where are the buzz and excitement of standing at the edge of the cliff? Money only supplies the ballast. My old belief, disgust and nausea with stock trading, comes from these dried-up negative thoughts. Is it a good idea to dwell on this, so I will engage with deeper experience and know the depths of its insanity? Maybe.

The belief comes from finding beauty, first in money, then in the balance between money and adventure. Is a calm, quiet view of Magnificence another level of Beauty?

Wednesday, February 21, 2024
I Love My Creations

I love my creations. Books, performances, and choreographies—that's all I've got. Is this egotistical and bad? Or bottom-line, basic-truth earthly and good?

I am also an excitement junky. And since fear goes with excitement, I'm also a fear junky. This has created lots of twisted avoidances on my path. Running tours, teaching folk dancing, even trading stocks are "easy" for me since, on one level, they are all forms of avoidance. They are born from my attitudes and can be seen as my creations, but somehow they are lesser. They shy away from expressing my essence, perhaps since they use the forms of others. But this is kind of a muddled explanation, and I don't truly know why they are lesser. Perhaps upbringing, my mother's values—she believed that artists are the greatest beings, and I believed her. I still do. Through countless twists and turns to avoid this truth, somehow, in the end, the belief in the high value of art and creation remains my bottom line.

So be it. The post-Covid cleansing question is: Can I follow through? Do I finally have the understanding and courage to promote my own values? And can I express myself by promoting creative work?

A "harmless" signal came from yesterday's trading, when I overdid my margin and ending up losing money. And strangely, after my initial fear and anger, I felt relieved, even thankful! I felt the blow would force me to give up trading and be free, liberated from my useless avoidance disease of trading wealth.

Of course, fame, money, prestige, all ultimately dribble away, so dreams or nightmares are not the answer. But nevertheless, in this temporary world, my creations remain important, since they express the central me.

See sales as giving to the audience: giving, offering my wares, books, performances, and choreos to others. The money I receive from their purchases underscores the value of my products, and thus confirms my value.

Selling (Offering) My Beauties

Spend my days editing, whittling, preparing my writing for market. (Add choreos and guitar videos, too.)

"Selling" is aggressive, whereas "offering" is (more) passive, but both are forms of giving.

The Magnificence of Clarity and Beauty of Order: Financial and Computer Fogs Have Lifted

Suddenly, it's all in order. The soggy mess underneath the financial fog has been cleared. Also, for the first time, not only are computers clear but, through understanding their inner workings, I see the possibility of feeling comfortable with them.

Excitement and fears, thrills and chills, may be fun. But they hide the beauty of clarity.

Slow

And the slow, slow, slow "Alhambra" is very good. I'm getting into, digging, fingers and fingernails into the meat and bones of each note like no one else in this world! I am making these discoveries. Of course, others can observe, listen, watch, enjoy, take part, part-ici-pate with me, in any way they want or can. All of us together. No problem. Total discovery and re-discovery, at every unique moment.

Thursday, February 22, 2024
Success

Success, followed by self-disgust, has often been my pattern.

The pattern has emerged again. This morning's self-disgust could indeed come from emotional success.

Even though part of me feels like a fool for losing money and playing the market in the first place, why not give myself credit for a victory, anyway? After all, I did feel "happy" when I lost it. A sign of impending health! Indeed, a loss can be a gain.

Friday, February 23, 2024
On Learning Hebrew

Listen. Do not translate (into English). Step into the sound. Become each word.

Doing Nothing Creates Motivation

No exercise yesterday, I took the day off—very difficult for me to do. But I did it. This morning I woke up feeling empty and stiff. But luckily and happily, right after coffee, I was hit by a wave of self-disgust. This feeling of nausea is an energy driver. I imme-diately jumped into my Hebrew study.

If I take a vacation, do nothing, even for a day, will I "easily and naturally" break out and do something? Does stopping ac-tually work?

So try: Let the do-nothing energy path do its magic.

Bless My Aches and Pains

In Hebrew the verb for "to paint" is *tzir*, which comes from toor meaning "tight, narrow, annoyance, anxious, pain," and "trouble." From this we get the word *tzuras*.

Tzir can also mean "painter, to draw," or if extended, "to create art." Or "artist." Thus, to be an artist means to feel *tzuras*, or pain.

This is an etymological way of saying: Bless my aches and pains. They are part of being an artist.

In life, there is no way to avoid pain. Evidently, since I want to be an artist, part of me must want or need the pain, since it is part of the process. It also means, or at least implies, that, at some level, everyone is an artist.

Evidently, squeezing tight, anxiety, and *tzuras* are sources of creation. So instead of trying to avoid them, why not happily dive into their welcoming misery-creating arms? After all, such em-braces sure help focus the mind.

Saturday, February 24, 2024
Flow

My job as a guitarist is to focus, concentrate, feel, touch the string, pluck it, and play one note, and listen to it (hear it. . . .

Then another note. . .and another. . .on and on. This smooth continuum, series of notes, creates flow. And flow is my job.

Victory, Energy, Inspiration

woke up this morning feeling overwhelmed and miserable. But I could choose victorious, energized, and inspired. After all, I've succeeded in fulfilling 95 percent of my February goal of modernizing my business. Stripe payments are (mostly) in order, and I (mostly) understand them; same with HubSpot emails: (mostly) in order; and I (mostly) understand how HubSpot works. Pinnacle Studio imports work, and I've even added Photoshop.

Mostly I've conquered my computer and come up with a new attitude: I'm competent with computers, can handle them, figure things out, and all I need is patience, persistence, and hard work. This is not only a computer breakthrough but a major emotional and attitudinal shift, basically a total victory!

Can I really choose to change my emotions and old habits, move from an overwhelmed misery to an attitude of victory, energy, and inspiration? Yes. But it's tough.

Winning inspires me to do more! A winning attitude means defeat; losing is about learning something new.

Sunday, February 25, 2024

I'm adding one hour of knees (legs) and computer study to my daily ritual/routine.

Also considering Polish and folk singing.

Study gives me distance, perspective, and detachment.

Somehow this morning my mind is clear, calm, directed, and peaceful. Could it be because my knees (legs) and my computer are now organized and part of my daily routines? Even folk singing stepped in with close to an hour of singing old songs. First time in months.

Writing is also different: little to no effort. Feels like I'm taking dictation. I write by hand in the morning, then enter it into my computer.

Guitar: Playing Classical Guitar Like A Folk Singer

Classical guitar may still have its place. But where?

This morning I'm playing classical guitar, and thinking, like a folk singer. What does that mean?

Playing classical guitar like a folk singer, thinking like a folk singer, is such a big deal. I've always felt totally comfortable singing folk songs, performing them, and leading group singing with them. It's relaxing, easy, lots of fun, even funny (note fun-knee: Could my knee get better with this realization?).

Since thinking like a folk singer is joyful, this could mean that playing classical guitar like a folk singer is a doorway to joy?

Is this a miracle in the making after so many years of search and struggle? I'm always looking for miracles, hoping for miraculous answers and events. Maybe it's part of being Jewish.

It also could be part of my inner habit of following my personal self-diminishment program, of attributing/giving the credit for self-development through persistence and hard work to "others," to outside forces, to so-called "miracles" rather than giving myself credit for all the years of persistence, sticking to it, never giving up the dream. Whatever the reason, I'm happy and hopeful today. Let's see where it leads.

Can I really give myself credit, say I did it rather than put it God's hands and say He did it through His miraculous powers? Is

God my "excuse" for avoidance, for running away, avoiding my own powers?

Of course, obviously, God is in charge of the universe and everything that happens. But (maybe) one of His commandments is that I'm in charge of myself and must take responsibility for my own powers, the ones He gave me. "It's your decision, Jim. I just run the universe. I'm glad to give you a hand and help out. But ultimately, and I use this word as the Supreme Power, it's your decision."

So what have I decided? Until now, I have striven to diminish and even deny my powers such as persistence, courage, love, the ability to make things happen, and such. But maybe, as of today, that's changing.

Shall I start by taking credit for this amazing mental turn and development of playing classical guitar like a folk singer?

Truth is that I love the power, beauty, joy, and magnificence of classical music and classical guitar, but I just have not been able to express it. (Jumping the gun a bit, but. . .now that I'm a folk singer, will I be able to?)

Monday, February 26, 2024
Choose Hope

This morning I rose with the following thoughts: Getting older, I find myself detaching, stepping out, slowly releasing myself from society. Is this good, bad, or a natural progression? Is stepping out of life, preparing for the afterlife, a preparation-for-the-future age thing? It feels somewhat sad, but also peaceful and right. Good, bad, or natural and normal?

Knowing that long-range, over centuries and time, nothing I

do or say will ever be remembered means that long-range, over time, nothing is important. Is this true? Or just another face of despair? Does death exist? Is it permanent? Or is there more?

I hope there's more. Having hope is a better way to live. But is hope right? It comes back to attitude and choice. I have the power to choose. I could choose hope. Whether hope is right or not, I'll never know. But it sure feels better!

Life of Mr. Abs Solar Plexus

How do I achieve the state of hope?
First, replace transient small "r" with big, long-lasting "R."
Give up belief in body and mind as Reality; then give up belief in events as Reality.
Focus on (a permanent hello to) Mr. Abs Solar Plexus, center of the energy-giving universe.

Sleeping with the Guitar

Fernando Soring my "Etude 12" way up the folk song ladder in Carnegie Hall, stepping my way from rung to rung, from center stage to highest balcony floor where sits the teenage me listening to Pete Seeger and the Weavers. Indeed, the pinnacle. Crossing over. . .into the audience energy tent. Or should I fall asleep with the guitar in my hands? Dozing (sleeping) in front of the audience: comfort or resistance? Where will this lead?

Tuesday, February 27, 2024
Email Freedom: Freedom To Be Funny and Poetic

Imagine if I could write loose, funny emails for tours, like my Monday folk dance class emails. In order to write them like those,

I would have to "not care." In other words, I'd be detached and free. Am I ready to do this for tours? Yes! Imagine, fun level tour emails! Wow. A big step. Freedom to be funny—and poetic!

Where does guitar fit in? What is now the purpose of playing? It is to teach me something through my hands—and fingers. What about "Alhambra" and the other classical pieces? I had no fun or joy, only pain and *tzuras*, and suffered practicing them since I felt compelled, forced, to play them fast. (This so I could play them "like the masters," which means like others.) I was a slave to speed.

But no longer. Those days are gone. So maybe now my hands are ready to teach me, or rather release me, to be funny and poetic.

I finished my February mode. March is coming up. Start practicing this attitude today.

Wednesday, February 28, 2024
Ups and Downs Are Creative

Should I milk my downs as creative sources, dive into their richness? Or avoid them, use my energy to dispel them?

What are the benefits? Well, first, I create something.

For the last, I create nothing—but on a narrow, forced-march, balanced path.

Evidently, the first is better. But I'm afraid I'll bore others with the constant rain of negativity. Still, although the pain of negative stuff may not feel good, it is a creative source. Fear and pain force me to create. And I like to create. That's the payoff.

So dive into the negative. It too has its pluses and rewards. Besides, on the positive side, there's a big market for death, fear, and depression. Why not milk it?

Guitar:

The ritual habit of mindless, rote, warm-up scales and legatos starts me off, gets me in the mood. So there's a plus to mindlessness.

Thursday, February 29, 2024

This marks just about four years since the beginning of Covid. Time to move on to something funny and poetic, to write in a new fun and poetry style. (The Covid period is over.) And play guitar that way, too.

"Give up" tours in the old way. See what happens.

The Fun and Poetry Alhambra Fingers

I may have gone as far as I can with moan and groan. Perhaps Covid days and the Covid lifestyle have run their course. The bell has cracked, and it's time to move on. Seems nothing has changed in my guitar playing over the years except I have a greater acceptance of myself. I am comfortable with slow and fast—and all modes. And great clarity has come to my "Alhambra" fingers. Which nods them into fun and poetry.

Of course, this is a giant internal shift. I have to admit it. And my "Alhambra" is perfect!

Friday, March 1, 2024

I'm angry and impatient over HubSpot. And I don't even need it! (Watch out for both emotions, especially impatience.)

There's no reason to be disturbed over HubSpot. The program is no longer necessary or that important; and, over the long term, I won't be paying for it again since my tours-business hopes, desires, and shape have changed. So there is no rush. HubSpot learning could be a mere "hobby."

Sure, I'll follow through with calls to Joe and Tim, After all, I've gone this far. But no reason to be angry or impatient.

I don't want happiness and amazement at my arrival in this new land to hold me back from walking in further. Dwell in wonder for a while.

CHAPTER SEVEN

Funny and Poetic

Friday, March 1, 2024

March is about getting used to living in this funny and poetic land. But the next path must be an adventure. Standing still does not keep me happy for long. Although I love the satisfaction that comes from conquest and victory, still my blood and dreams only quicken with a fresh adventure in sight. So what will it be?

Saturday, March 2, 2024
Ab-normal Month of March

Play guitar with focus on my abs. It works! This obsession on abs will become my March ab-session. Create a habit of focusing on them in all activities and places. Normalize this focus.

Sunday, March 3, 2024
Persistence Wins the Day

Could tightening my abs become a pleasant sensation that I look forward to feeling? Yes. The benefits are obvious.

Paradoxically, could there be a relaxed / tightened, constant / consistent abs? A universal Ab?

It works, in "Alhambra." I've been on the cusp of this for year, but I never gave into it because I thought it was wrong. No longer. Now I know abdominal dominance is right.

Monday, March 4, 2024
The Illusion Is Part of the Fun

It's important that others think my work is important, because their belief (and acceptance) help make my work more important to *me*.

I'm entering a new world by returning to my old one. But naked, stripped of old gear, I am returning clean and fresh.

So what's so bad? I'm a bit sad that HubSpot has failed. But with the use of PDFs, letters, and links, I really don't need it. Having better emails has also had no effect on business or sales. Basically, I'm "artistically" disappointed: Learning HubSpot, with all the frustrations and *tzuras* involved, was vaguely a fun challenge, and even a wahoo experience when things went right. However, I'd have to call it a month wasted. . .a necessary prelude to something else.

· Am I back to facing the process of promoting my books, folk dance videos, even guitar videos? Could that process be enjoyable?

Of course, I could also suffer *with* my fun. That might make it even more fun.

I'm ready for a total return, but on a different level. Am I fooling myself? Maybe. But *the illusion is part of the fun.*

I could start with the illusion of practicing for a real concert. Even give myself an illusion date and video the performance I give in the living room.

My journal is also important. Believing this illusion will help me promote volume three of the Covid trilogy.

What about folk dancing? Time to make videos of my new choreographies and prepare a second choreography book!

Wednesday, March 6, 2024

Woke up with usual feeling of being lost, battered, stabbed, uncertain, and uncentered. "Chaos" and "chaotic" are good words for this state of mind. Evidently, I wake up in chaos. I hate chaos. I love order and harmony. My job is to re-establish it. This morning, I had once again drifted off center; I had forgotten my job. Hub-Spot was a short-term distraction. But now my head's together.

So I'm focused again, I'm back. Reading Hebrew first thing in the morning centers me—in self and God. Are they the same? Yes. (Note: No secular shame, often called "embarrassment," in saying the word "God." Another victory.)

Hebrew, followed by guitar playing, are another Yes for the centered life.

Chaos is the Enemy of Happiness

Chaos breaks body and mind apart; order and focus make it flow. When all my Stripe tour credit payments are in order, and I view the Beauty of order, a sense of peace, security, and happiness emerges.

Tight Abs and Relaxation: Hard Meets Soft

Hard can't exist without soft.

A warm, relaxed feeling comes when tight abs send their energy flow into arms, hands, and legs. The soft limb, limber and lovely, is fed and nurtured by hard, tight abs.

For the first time in my life, I am not nervous when opening a folk dance class. Where am I? What does this mean, if anything?

It could be a strange wonderful place.

Thursday, March 7, 2024

Strange: no down this morning. After no folk dance teaching pre-fear yesterday. First time. The old constant pre-performance anxiety fear just clicked off, stopped, vanished, fell away, disappeared, was beside the point. I'd like to feel this means something, is a place for me, that something positive is happening and might also flood into guitar.

Could focus on abs be part of it? (I hesitate to analyze it too much.) After all, abs are where fear resides. By focusing on it, I'm saying that, since I'm there already, sitting in the home of fear, focusing on it is beside the point.

Saturday, March 9, 2024
Ego and Beauty

HubSpot is 90–95 percent done; so is Stripe. I'm 90–95 percent modernized. I shall glow in the pellucid moment of victory, at least for awhile. But I'll soon be moving on to videos and more. It's never really *over*, since all is flow and change.

Enjoy the pleasant tension of tight (tightening my) abs.

Ego is in the fingers. Beauty is in the thumb.

I have tremendous fingers.

I also have a tremendous thumb.

My struggle has been about fighting off ego, or at least putting it in its proper place behind Beauty.

Without someone in charge, a leader, there is chaos, conflict, and darkness. Just as Betzalel, chief biblical artisan of the Tabernacle (Ark of the Covenant), stood in the shadow of God, so let my guitar fingers stand in the happy shadow of my thumb.

Sunday, March 10, 2024
Ego and AIO

Hebrew is not a pretty language. It is a tough, hard, flinty, desert-blown one, rock-hard and enduring, built for endurance, like God and the Jews.

Tuesday, March 12, 2024
Into the Flow

Life is flow, constant change.

So, is progress real? Or an illusion?

Of course, *technological* progress is real. But what about moral progress? Right or wrong? Any progress on that front?

Is it a constant human struggle to do what's right?

And what *is* right?

The path is so often confusing. Does emptiness really exist? Is boredom an illusion, a false vacuum? Will the Messiah come, or he is already here? Perhaps the Messiah is now.

Maybe there *is* no place to go: We are here already.

If true, is that disappointing and unmotivating? No reason to grow or improve. Unless, of course, growth and improvement are goods-in-themselves. Which happily, I believe they are!

The *process* puts you back into the flow.

Friday, March 15, 2024
Love (of) My Business

Susan is worried about the complications of the Peru trip. She asked lots of questions about the internal flights of tour. I'll answer them in an email. Or I may even call her.

Details, business. *Love* my business!

First time I've ever used the word "love" with it. This along with no pre-performance anxiety before teaching my folk dance class.

Will love replace fear? Is that where I'm heading?

Fear and excitement often walk together. They are twins. But love is another dimension. Metaphysical, somewhat other-worldly, it is also earthy and concrete. As such it is in business.

In business I mix the physical with the metaphysical, the worldly with the unworldly, the earthly with the extra-terrestrial.

Art and work blend in love of business.

Is *love* of business my salvation in love form? It could be.

Moments later: The voice of doubt rises. Am I kidding myself?

But the word *love* did come up spontaneously. And I *would* love to love my business. Does love make it happen?

Loving the Details

This means I'd be combining business with my others loves: Hebrew, languages, guitar, folk dancing, writing, exercising, art, and creation.

Carrying this love into the *details* of business means growing a pleasantness of answering emails, paying bills, advertising, promotions, and stuff like that.

This would remove the pressure to finish projects, assemble details and such, since love would be a constant presence. Of course, this state would approach perfection, a rare moment indeed. Still, rare does not make it untrue.

No question my business makes *other* people happy. That's a good start.

But business demands often annoy and overwhelm me. Isn't that a negative mental condition, a thought over which I have control?

And the truth is, my business doesn't *have* to annoy and overwhelm me. They're mere attitudes I choose to have! I could choose differently. I could choose to enjoy, play, design, laugh, banter, sing, dance, and love my business!

Now that's a challenge to take up! And with several years of the Covid cleansing process now finished, I'm ready to take it.

Saturday, March 16, 2024
Total Pleasure Pavane

My first total pleasure: "Pavane in C."

It began with a courageous redirection.

A pledge of sales, promotion, and advertising. Which meant: standing up for myself, in public, in many ways, for my many things. An act of (personal) courage. A new choreo book, and my journal.

I also chose not to burden and distract myself by adding more tours—to Turkey, Croatia, and Portugal—unless I can find, and hire, someone or someones to do it with and for me: Anthea, Ventsi, Lee O., Lee F., Zack, Cathie. Together, us. Promo all my things as a united entity, one united expression of many aspects.

As for guitar, just luxuriate and enjoy it. (Speed, tempo, all beside the point.) Let the sensual pleasure roll.

Engulf glory. Embrace the beautiful miracle of inner freedom.

Could day-trading stocks be the best training for writing, and becoming an entrepreneur? Education through the mystery of unexpected bumps.

Sunday, March 17, 2024
The Guitar Spot

I am a writer. The proof is that I am writing.

Use the deep "C Pavane" as model.

Can fast and slow merge into clarity? Can loud and soft do the same? That is the road to "better." Give up the stopping point, the death and frozen place, of "best."

Go to the fresh muscular place where the cells have never been before.

A possibly better finger muscular focus place exists. Clarity brings light, the road to the better.

It is a place of belief, faith, and no doubt. I know I am there, briefly. But the poison clouds of doubt drift in, and gray covers the light.

Practice believing in this guitar spot. Practice giving up doubt.

Monday, March 18, 2024
Benefits of Imperfection: Aim for Better and Imperfect

Best and perfection equal death.

Better and imperfection equal life.

So to embrace life, give up perfect and best, and dive into imperfect better.

If I embrace that, I can do just about anything. And it's funny, too. Poetic and funny was the direction I wanted to go in. I can do it by being the imperfect creature I am.

Protect the Imperfection Route

How to do this?

To begin with, nobody should be looking or listening, which means no one is there to criticize.

Criticism is, as usual, my big fear. And it is reasonable and right to be afraid of it: Criticism can destroy you.

So where do I practice imperfection? I can't expect total, even any, public acceptance.

Maybe privately is the only place. But that's okay, it's a start. Maybe a finish as well; that's okay, too.

Is the drive toward perfection merely a subtle attempt to avoid criticism? Maybe.

The imperfection road is broken when you take a close look.

Who needs it? Yet it is the only road we have, the only one to travel. Only attitude can smooth the bumps.

Wednesday, March 20, 2024
Black Cloud Peeks in To Say Hello

Another blast of morning wind has knocked new holes in my old goals. It is simply another black cloud nightmare reappearing? Yes. Transient and passing? Yes. (Again so hard to believe in its illusory power.)

So pay no attention to this blowhard. Go past it, and do what's right.

What's right? My daily ritual, glorious routines, and making plans to follow it again.

The road back.

Thursday, March 21, 2024

The purpose of ritual is to control fear. And it works!

Do I have a morning ritual? Yes.

I began with a blinding headache. This means I know I'm angry about something. I feel pushed around by internal changes. Suddenly, I hear: *Give up Hebrew* (for awhile, I hope). *It has served its purpose.* (I hope not.) *Replace it with serious writing—of stories (á la* Perelman). *And add some folk dance video editing.*

Does this mean change the order of my ritual?

I'm upset, overwhelmed, mad, puzzled, and confused. Maybe nothing should change. But now, my next direction is slower, less and less, but deeper.

I'm moving from scattered to focused and compressed.

Perhaps I'm already there but don't recognize it. Perhaps my morning ritual is already my warm-up for writing. Note: It includes journal writing, noting thoughts and things in my journal, which always feel like calls from above, vital, a must.

Perhaps this morning routine *is* my unique and natural writing warm-up. Perhaps I've been doing it all along but didn't recognize it as such.

Power, Retreat, Return

I felt the power of my focus on abs, and the thought that I can handle anything. Then Mr. Fear popped up. Frightened like a mouse, I retreated into a panic hole, tail between my legs. I wailed, *My body is too weak, stiff, and frail, I can't take it, I'll fall apart, I'll be injured, hurt, if I move or exercise too much, push too hard.* And I stayed in that hole, trembling, for a week. But on the eighth day, when I arose, a ray of awareness crept in.

Now I'm conscious of this mental trick. So I crept out of my hole. The weather, although not perfect, looks better.

Saturday, March 23, 2024
Redefining Sales and Business

Perfect my craft, get better. That's the next stage.

I need visceral goals and plans—gutsy, tough, and challenging.

All activities are equally important, but only attitude makes them so.

Focus on love, fascination, and the wonders of tours and travel. Do not focus on numbers.

Are there wonders and fascinations in my CEO position?

To find them, I have to first know that a growth in the number of travelers happens incidentally, on the side, almost by accident, and mostly beyond my control. The heart of sales is focusing on each traveler one at a time.

So I need to give up my ancient desire, along with its noxious hope, of getting more customers. This useless, pushy, and pompous definition of sales and business was a killer of spirit.

Redefining sales and business as a focus on love, respect, and companionship would be a giant leap in healthy attitude. It totally fits my post-Covid mindset.

An amazing Spring. Amazing what I'm saying and feeling, experiencing and solidifying, in my journal. And another wonder is, it isn't a wonder anymore. It feels vaguely normal. After a week's rest and veering, the ocean liner has turned, heading in another direction.

Natural Advertising and Promotion (Finding the Real Me)

I'd like others to know about my process, what I'm going through, what I've experienced. Writing clarifies my mind. That's why I write in my journal

I also want others to know about what's happening in my mind, how I do things, personal adventures of change and growth.

Writing my journal is visceral, easy, and necessary, an existential must, a fluid self-advertising and promotional campaign without self-conscious effort, normal, and born of an inner need.

I'm so happy to discover this! It means, somewhere deep in my core, I *do* want to advertise and promote. I *do* want others to know. (At least about me!) I'm now aware of the reason I need to advertise and promote! It expresses heartfelt efforts of the real me.

So there's no more reason to hate, despise, or feel forced to advertise and promote. Quite a realization and victory. Big league stuff.

Sunday, March 24, 2024
The Great Unworthy

The great unworthy feeling shames me into wanting to expand, grow, learn, improve. These feelings of worthlessness, shame, and self-disgust mean my "just-do-it" energy is rising. Motivation will soon be here.

So I need to use these feelings. I can't help but do so. No choice. . .or rather, my only choice.

I feel lucky to have these unworthy feelings, because motivation is glorious!

When standing on my right leg, I felt shame focusing so totally and completely on my abs for balance. But it worked!

Am I ashamed of my power? Do I fear it? Yes. Well, my focus on abs is exhausting—but it is Truth.

It works for "Alhambra."

In social situations, too: Remember the abs.

It also created the "forever" feeling. When standing on my right leg, focused completely on my abs, I felt I could stay standing "forever." A heavenly feeling.

Are abs related to heaven, to heavenly power?

Obligations from Don't to Do

I used to think, if I didn't want to do something, there was a good reason for it but I didn't yet know what it was. So to find out, I chose *not* to do it. My philosophy was "Just don't do it!" *Say no* became an adventure in learning about how I thought, a path to wisdom through rebellion.

Now that I'm older and a bit wiser, I know the right path for me—what to do, what's good for me, and others.

But in spite of this self-knowledge, I still don't want to do many of these good things.

So, since now I know the right path to health, happiness, and fulfillment, my philosophy has changed. I've gone from "just *don't* do it" to "*just do* it!"

Monday, March 25, 2024

"A coffee cup chill of Hebrew satisfaction." This sentence is deep with *sentir*, or Latin feeling, and a nice feeling it is.

But good feeling or bad feeling, it's just *a* feeling, a passing cloud, and *not* a direction, path, or purpose. As such, acknowledge, say hello, wave goodbye, and move on. Finish my task, routine, or ritual. Do the full hour of language study no matter what.

And I did. I kept moving and finished the hour. A victory over a (this time, positive) feeling.

Annette and her dance group know my "Ne Klepeci." But they didn't know "El Pastor," or any of my other dances. And there is no reason that they should, since no one (including me) has ever shown them these folk dance creations.

Do I really want to share my creations? Sure, in the past, fears, time restraints, and other excuses kept me from teaching them, spreading my gone-public wings. But now things are different. It's post-Covid time. I'm cleansed of past fears, "Dare I?" questions, and walking the right path in *just do it* mode.

Does this path now reveal an obligation to bring my folk dance creations, Jim Gold choreos, to the public? (And what about my books, or even classic guitar?)

Does the focus on abs give the mental and physical tool, the skill and power, to do it? Is that why it is appearing now?

Transitions

"Alhambra" succeeds with abs and thumb. Success is still a fresh wound, a minor trauma. But I *can* do it! I just have to get used to it. Transitions happen slowly.

It's sad giving up, losing the old life with its stiff, stunted ways. Even though her (or is it *his*) attitudes kept me down, at least it was familiar. Full of complaints, negativity, and lack of support, a miserable friend, but a friend, nevertheless. Now she / he / it is fading and will, I hope, soon be gone. Whipsawed with a sad happiness and a happy sadness.

Wednesday, March 27, 2024
Small Pleasures along the Way

The happy surprise: I can read Hebrew mostly with *nikkudim*. Amazed and happy. But so what? Be amazed for my ten seconds.

Excitement, like the fear it engenders, can both be obstacles to feeling. Feel them if you like, bask in their glory of accomplishment—but not for too long. After the rise and fall, move on (quickly if possible) to follow the good-path rituals of daily routine.

Each guitar finger and folk-dance leg must establish its own individual abdominal connection first, before all fingers and legs they connect can be united in alliance and allegiance.

This is done through loud, strong touch and pluck, and strong push, focused stretch, or squat.

Thursday, March 28, 2024
Thumb and Index Run the "Alhambra" Show

There's a certain point, probably after fifteen minutes of warm-ups, where the body and its fingers *yearn* to break free, expressed as *go faster.*

On the border of loss, where one never gives up the battle, I'm cracking the abs and index code. Dropped from four fingers to two.

How easy then to double the speed, go fast—marvelous discovery found only after sinking to the black bottom of the barrel where, in the rich nutrient depths of giving up, dirt, humus, and strange plants survive, thrive, and grow.

Believe this discovery breakthrough: Turns out that my ring and middle fingers follow the index leader almost as mindless slaves, by-products, AI robots, afterthoughts. *Thumb and index run the "Alhambra" show.*

Friday, March 29, 2024
Balance

Be aware of "too much enjoyment." I don't want to fall into the "amazement and awe" trap. It shuts me down, stops me, and I end up doing nothing more. I have to be aware of it, but not give into it.

(If I do, the opposite, namely, the down energy time called depression, will soon arrive.)

Stay on the good ritual-routine path. This creates balance. And balance is best.

It's scary, awe-some, how focus on abs, as the center of truth, works every time. (Abs as gutsy, All-Is-One connection.)

Does focus on abs include the heart? Well, why not? Abs

include the stomach, center of fear and excitement. They are also near the heart, which can unite all in love. As part of my focus on abs, try including the heart. It would unite fear and excitement and transform their energy into love. A beautiful idea.

The etymology of "awe" is Hebrew *ire*, fear. "Awesome" is God-fearing at its best. Along with its sister, excitement, it's the kind of fear I can use.

Can I be resurrected on this gutsy connection? Well, why not? After all, tomorrow is Easter; it's resurrection time. And Passover is about freedom. You can't have a good resurrection without freedom.

Behind all the cultural gobbledygook, Easter and Passover are the same. (Maybe we should have seder now that I have something meaningful to add.)

New Leaf Journal is all about resurrection, freedom, and starting fresh every day; it's about Easter, Passover, and seize-the-moment.

If I could believe this deep in my heart, I would push it relentlessly as part of my core belief. It would justify my whole life and give me a reason to advertise and promote (in these remaining years).

(Note the sudden sadness of "in these remaining years." Why did it suddenly come up? Aha! An old negative friend arising in new form of put-down, and subtle attempt to diminish the power of a great idea. Negative thoughts about death and loss are "realistic" new forms of put-downs for older people, a dark cloud of so-called "valid" negativity to dampen, soften, and oppose the light, new ways for seniors to avoid enthusiasm, growth, and personal development. In other words, They are a good, devious excuse for doing absolutely nothing, for opposing Easter/Passover hope.)

Sunday, March 31, 2024
Polytheism to Monotheism

Why the headache, anger, and ultimate sadness behind them? I must be losing something.

And I am. I'm giving up my old friend Mr. Fear. He is leaving on the next train; he is going out the window, dying, draining into the distance of ancient memories. And I'm sad, in mourning, almost crying—angry, too, as my old motivator disappears into the night. Will he be gone forever, never to motivate my guitar playing again?

Who will replace him? His twin brother Excitement, with his opposite personality, will, I'm sure, motivate me for a short while. But even he, in his old incarnation, is too attached to his family. When he helps me, I'm always reminded of his brother.

So I need a new way of looking at these twins.

Since they both live in my abs, maybe I can unite them, at least in concept. I can rename them: Universal as a first name, Energy as second. Universal Energy.

Plurality to unity, polytheism to monotheism, union, oneness, love, all-is-one, and all living in my abs.

Is this merely mental trick to fool my mind into moving forward? Maybe. But who cares as long as it works?

And at least for today, it does.

Monday, April 1, 2024
Abs Can Be Fun

Connection with the Universal Energy can be fun!

Dare I even think of such a thing? (Totally new idea! What a daring and wonderful post-Covid conclusion.)

How did I even arrive here?

This morning, after my usual coffee and Bernice breakfast preparation, I followed with my usual Hebrew *Yanshuf* reading. Then I saw the word *avor* used as "for."

That's when the ball started rolling. I wrote, "Abs are the bridge, the crossing point, the *avor*."

Then I moved to guitar. Warmed up, then to "Alhambra" as usual:

Abs and bass—where the nutrients are. Thumb acts as 90 percent representative, while fingers remain outside the farm basement windows, shining in with 10 percent.

Easing into the abdominal burden. A burden is responsibility. But responsibilities can be fun! (Now that's a totally new one. Thank you, Bernice!) This means focus on abs—responsibility can be fun! (Another totally new one.)

Dare I even think such a thing? Connection with universal energy through my abs. . .and consider it fun? What a concept and marvelous development!

Tuesday, April 2, 2024
Aiming for Pleasant, Even, Steady, Balanced

Arms and leg hanging off the abs, like sticks.

Arms for guitar. Legs for walking, running, dancing. Loose and relaxed, with focus on abs.

Aim for the pleasant realm. Stay even, steady, and balanced. Don't be swayed by miracles and amazement.

Really? Aim for the pleasant and even? What about excitement and its handmaiden fear? Yes—I'll lose miracles and amazement, but also downs and depression.

Do I really want this? Yes. It's totally different. Plus, regarding the up-and-down life with its high and low emotions, I've had my fill of that.

Here comes a headache: the usual anger and sadness over losing old attitudes. But nevertheless, losing, giving it up, seems inevitable. I have to accept it. I'll have to get used to it.

I'm sick over the loss—at least for now.

Wednesday, April 3, 2024
New View of Art

Slipping into a new view of art.

A kaleidoscope, a medieval tapestry of Jim Gold International tours. But is this, can this be, a worthy, lasting work of art?

My old view was that a company or business is transient, while a work of art is permanent. But really, even though a company or business may last only a lifetime, how long does so-called "artistic" permanence last? True, medieval tapestries are still viewed in museums, as are ancient Roman and Greek statues, and even neolithic tools are displayed.

But how long is the "permanence" even of civilizations? A few thousand, even many thousand, years isn't really that long. Isn't the idea of permanence a silly belief? After all, nothing really lasts. Only God is permanent.

So maybe I should rethink the idea of the tour business. Why not a kaleidoscope, a tapestry of tours? Very pretty, indeed. And even if for only one lifetime.

Strange Connections

Strange things are happening. I went to the eye doctor yesterday. The family history of glaucoma is creeping up on me. Time to start taking an eye drop medication. I left the optometrist's office feeling quite down but also thankful for modern medicine, that curative eye drops exist, and that my situation can be "easily" handled.

Yet I still felt somewhat defeated. Soon a strange yet somewhat familiar panic took over. Suddenly, all my post-Covid progress dribbled away, vanished, disappeared, I was left with nothing but emptiness and fear. Return to the old neighborhood.

That evening, a pain behind my left knee reappeared. But it somehow felt "different." I sensed it had much to do with the optometrist visit, my eyes, glaucoma, my mother, can't function, rest, sickness, weak, frail—old-neighborhood stuff.

I tried to resurrect my confidence by playing guitar. "Alhambra," of course. Here's the strange jumble I wrote:

The male principle—thumb—coming in strong, dominant, tough, and kind. Questionable thumb dominance over the second string, the last straw. Connection between thumb, second string, and left knee.

Played "Alhambra" again: The dusk of doubt and questioning—dusking, dusking, and with each dusk playing each entrance as thumb and second string improve (dusk out); so does left knee.

The happy (pleasant) entrance of a powerful, kind thumb. A king covering, protecting, embracing, hugging the tender second string of left knee. In kindness and strength it reigns.

Now it's just about there: 90 percent. One more day.

So powerful and amazing. But do not slip into awe.

Thursday, April 4, 2024
The Tour Business Puzzle: Sales/Business/Social Director Personality

I wonder why I stay in the tour business. It isn't fun, like folk dance teaching. It isn't intellectually stimulating, like Hebrew, learning HubSpot and Adobe Premiere or other studies. It can be financially rewarding, but I don't need the money the way I used to. (But getting money is fun.) It is something of an organizational challenge. But again, that is mostly lots of work, time, and effort, and I wouldn't call it fun.

Being and becoming the CEO of my JGI company is a partial challenge with lots of paperwork, which I might pass off as "interesting," but I would never call it fun either.

And yet I stay in the tour business. I'm even trying to expand it. Why? Is there some kind of attraction I'm missing?

So far folk dance teaching, with its performance and social director aspects, has all the fun.

Maybe it's the sales aspect. After all, sales are a form of performance and social directorship. And I can rationally allow myself to sell tours, since I can and do make money from them. With tours, even a lot of money is possible. They also have a worldwide potential for growth, excitement, and more money.

Are sales fun? Formerly, my background and upbringing would never have allowed me to say yes. But post-Covid life is different. I'm moving past my upbringing.

Performing, people, acting like a social director (with social organizing, organizational skills), having fun kibbitzing with people . . .maybe I *do* have a sales personality. Maybe acknowledging, liking, even loving that quality and gift is the missing tour business link.

Playing alone is fun art.

Playing with others is even more fun business.

Friday, April 5, 2024
Mind Control

Dark thoughts pass through my mind as I focus on the aches in my morning body.

Dark thoughts disappear, transform into light thoughts, as I change focus and focus on playing my guitar.

Focus counts! Mind control is so important. After all, the mind contains "only" thoughts. And they come and go (Carlos the Cloud passing through the night).

As the dark and light clouds of feeling swirl, battering mind and body, good weapons (ideas) to use in the battle for mind control are: Move on, look ahead, just do it, always improve. Stick to them, keep focusing (on them), and eventually they will win.

Saturday, April 6, 2024
Life Philosophy

Never finished, always improving, with short rests between victories and defeats: I want to remember and live by this philosophy.

As to public and private (my own) reactions to my activities (what I do): Positive and negative, victories and defeats, can be *misleading* (Twyla Tharp's word). Disregard up, down, sideward, and backward swings of the road to improvement.

Stay on the good path no matter what.

Sunday, April 7, 2024

Three good things a day:

1. I want to keep a Good Things Journal. As for negatives, they're easy. I'm already good at them, too good.

2. Deep, slow, focused Hebrew (slow equals fast in the depth world).

3. Idea: Warm up directly in front of the audience. Make it part of my concert, or dance class. (It takes about 10–15 minutes

to warm up, and 20 minutes to reach the magic land of transformation where the workday world vanishes, slow equals fast, beauty begins to seep into the soul.

Monday, April 8, 2024

Discouraged about Israel. Political discouragement, distress, depression, are the same as personal discouragement, distress, depression, and are dealt with the same way: Dive into the next project. Just do it.

Guitar

I leave my wounded index finger with you, my audience. Take care of it; hold, love, and embrace it. Then we'll be safe and secure. And we will be healed.

Terror has resided in my index finger. By giving it to the audience (sharing my terror), I am losing it.

And it only took eighty-six years.

I've broken the protective wall. Now, somehow, it feels as if I'm inured to criticism.

Uniting with the audience has put me in a safe (calm, quiet, peaceful) and beautiful place.

(Note the word *inure*, etymologically related to Latin *opus* ("work"), "opera," Hebrew *aver*.)

Energy Camouflage

Later: Leaving to teach folk dancing, feeling empty, drained, a sick-to-my-stomach moment and bordering on nausea.

Pre-performance nervousness used to reside in my stomach.

In losing my fear, am I also losing (giving up) my energy?

Or is this nausea a prelude to a new beginning, a fresh form of fear-replacement energy coming in, camouflaged in old clothing?

Tuesday, April 9, 2024
Heroic Old Man

Heroic old man: Can there be such a thing?

Well, why not? And if not, maybe I can start it.

How does an old man return to dancing and choreography? (I hate to *call* myself an old man, but I am.) Maybe I can find something heroic in this return.

How? First, fight on the side of good against an evil enemy. What am I fighting against? The forces of frailty, decay, stagnation, darkness, depression, despair, and death. What am I fighting for? Creativity, invention, health, uplift, radiance, and life. In this endless fight, I'd be a hero at any age, even an old one.

An April Adobe Premiere Pro Art and Business Calling

What's my present state? On the positive side: I ran a great folk dance class last night, I'm choreographing slow, naturally, bit by bit, and videos are on their way; Adobe Premier Pro is ready to roll (even though I'm still in the infant learning stages), Hebrew is flowing, and so is guitar performing. All good stuff.

On the negative side, extreme aches and pains in my legs after dancing last night. (Nothing new there.) But I also sense the extremes of these aches are a result of "sitting" for two months learning computer programs.

What to do? Start training again.

I'm returning to the workday world as a dancer and choreographer. (I've never said *that* before!) I'll add guitar stuff as well.

Crossing the video line is s big deal.

I see myself making hundreds of videos over the next two years. Folk dancing, and guitar. (I even felt a slight churn of excitement and fear in my stomach!)

Guitar

Guitar vision: Performing before a video camera.

Closing the full circle. But I accept it all now; that's the difference.

Relish in the slow, but relish in fast, too.

Nothing has changed—but everything has changed!

Wednesday, April 10, 2024
Improve Legs

Immediate "laughable" negative thoughts emerge: At this age? Impossible. It's only downhill from here. Has anyone ever done this before? Can I be the first?

No matter what the answers, there is no choice but to try. (Twyla Tharp's books are my turn-around readings here.)

Guitar

Playing scales, arpeggios, even legato: Look into the audience. See past their eyes straight into their center.

Look into the soul of the audience, the individual soul of each member; send my vibrations to them.

If I give, share my pain, aches, and sorrows with them, will my struggles lessen, even go away? Could be.

Well, why not? I'm talking about a larger abs distraction, substituting a universal All-is-One (God) for my own "local" abs. (Here comes another negative for having a great idea: Dare lowly I use the word "God?" I'm not worthy. Or am I? *Voilá* this bit of laughable self-diminishment, but of course, on a higher level.)

Big Mama Me

When the index finger is connected to the audience, hidden power is found and released. That's what the tickle in my index finger means: hidden power about to explode. The rest-stroke *(apoyando)* scale power carries over to the free-stroke arpeggios. They are the same. Only their transfer of power is different—one through rest (relaxation), the other through freedom.

Hopefully, focus on the abs will come back, together with the audience, transformed as one grand universal *dantien* focus.

After this discovery, I fell into the most beautiful sleep. Such deep peace. Give in, explore, enjoy.

It's not even having the courage to play Bach's "Gavotte in D" slow and meaty. There's no choice. Slow, strong, and meaty is the only way left.

Friday, April 12, 2024
Fresh Motivation

I have found a fresh motivational source: the audience. This goes beyond "pleasing" them. It is more that I *am* the audience, and the audience is *me*. We are one. Since my goal is to improve, I know I always work, try to give my best to the audience. They push me beyond my limits, force me to be my best. In the process, I improve.

Note how, as a tour leader, I do things for my travelers I would never do for myself alone. I push beyond acceptable limits. Since I am their leader, they are depending on me to give them my best. As a performer, I rise to the task and do what it takes to accomplish the deed. And since all is one, I cannot improve alone. When I improve, they do as well. And it's all for the good.

Guitar

Dive right in from the very first second. But before I do: Take my pre-performance meds, the meds of meds-ition. How?

Gather the energy in my abs before I start, then spread and send it through my body, and into my hands, then spread its warmth and power into the world-audience. Do this. . .always.

Give my audience the best. And that desire pushes, forces, dynamites, me into elevation mode. It motivates me to go beyond my limits. I'll do anything, and I'll do everything, to give them my best. This may or may not please them. But that is their decision; their pleasure is beyond my control. But within my control is giving them my best, making my supreme effort.

And I will. It is simply in my nature to do so. Nothing else will satisfy me. (Note: When I do not give my best, do not make my maximum effort, I feel miserable after the show. I've cheated both my audience and myself. I had a chance to rise and experience glory, but I gave it up for the tasteless candy of ease, lack of effort. By choosing darkness over light, the result is always post-performance regret and misery.)

I know I'm at my best when I gather my energy, focus on the task at hand, drill into the desire to improve and bring it all to the audience.

Saturday, April 13, 2024

I'm sliding back to discouragement. Why? I'm feeling lots of pain in my body, the black face of it. Of course, I'm doing lots of good things: I restarted yoga, running, and added a warm-up squat-pulling-with-weights exercise that Rick gave me. But, oh, the pains! What do they mean? Oh, yes, I'm *advancing!* Yes, the pains hurt. But they are not injuring pains; they are growing pains. So I know I'm on the right track.

Innocuous daily aches and pains could be a call for discouragement or a call to do more. Being on the right track ("pain is weakness leaving the body") shows I'm growing, improving, expanding.

No question I *feel* the pain, but how to interpret it?

I *choose* the meaning.

So why not with my pledge to ever improve, see this pain as a positive sign, the "good pain" of growth and expansion?

How to reinterpret pain as good? How to make Mr. Pain and his partner, Mrs. Aches, my friends?

Guitar

Loving (and fucking) the Audience. She is a beauty.

Fucking means anger. I'm giving Audrey Audience my *angry best!* It also means I'm standing up for her, protecting her, the positive side of rage: "Audience, I cast my protective mantle over you." (That's what positive fucking is all about.)

It's positive rage that protects the weak and vulnerable. Use mine to heal and protect my audience. (Note: pains and aches make me angry. Thus do they reveal and bring out masculine healing and protective powers.)

Righteous rage as positive, right, and protective. *Righteous protective guitar playing.* Use it to heal myself and others.

Breaking My Records

My body ached everywhere; everything hurt. Hounded by doubt, I went to the gym anyway. . .and broke all my records!

Another proof that you can't trust your feelings too much. Another proof of follow your "Do What's Right" rituals.

Monday, April 15, 2024
Exploring

This sinking feeling into morning emptiness is because parts of my old identity are slipping away, and slowly being blown out of sight. What old parts? Artist, folk dancer, guitarist.

What new parts are on the horizon?

Video: videography with Adobe Premiere Pro, Hebrew, salesman and travel consultant ("agent") of normal, regular tours—an addition to folk dance tours.

Scary, and somewhat nauseous as I sink.

Results: For the guitar, audience, improvement, and all that other stuff doesn't matter anymore. Maybe this indifference or non-attachment is a good thing. (Are indifference and non-attachment the same? The first feels somewhat negative, the latter more positive. Evidently, whether you choose both or one or the other, you still need love, the quiet, peaceful kind.

Evidently, I no longer have to improve. It is beside the point. But I do like and want to explore. "Improvement" goes with work pressure, still good, but different. "Exploring" is a better word. It goes with curiosity.

Tuesday, April 16, 2024
Tread Water Creation "On The Spot"

The era of "on the spot" creation is dawning. How did this happen? I lost interest in practicing guitar. What to do? Tread water. Play even by rote. Keep practicing until something new happens. Just do it.

And I suddenly realized (hopefully for good) that, after years and years of personal pressure to play "Alhambra" fast, I finally know the only way I can play it is slow, meditative, exploring, luxuriating in each note. When I play it this way, "Alhambra" is mine!

True as well for Sor's "Etude Number 12." The audience, if any, will have to follow me. I am their leader. Also my folk dance classes. (Here I *do* have an audience.) Create my classes "on the spot." What fruits will a slow "Leyenda" bring?

Everything slow and original. Creation on the spot!

Wednesday, April 17, 2024

Fame and fortune are nice, but they are really not that important. Sometimes they can even be annoying. What *is* important?

So far I've got:

1. Lock into the present; change along with it.
2. Dive into the river of my Loves.
3. Flow gently.

This gives me complete freedom on guitar, and videos as well. (Even dancing.) What will I do with it?

Nothing has changed, but everything has changed.

I am (gingerly) taking the first leap into the post-Covid lifestyle. Once I'm here and it has been revealed, I can't go back to the old ways even if I try.

Friday, April 19, 2024
Entering the Granada Palace

The desire to return is strange, but, on the other hand, very familiar. Like visiting an old friend. I "want" to go backward as a guitarist, back to the old neighborhood. . .but I can't.

I miss it. . .but I can't return.

Here is a new and glorious place, a palace of victory and peace. I'm happy in this different residence. And it feels like the Alhambra palace in Granada.

I'm also about ready to "get back to work." It means integrating Adobe Premier Pro videos with HubSpot emails, and Stripe payments. (And adding website forms.) Seems that videos are the last link—aiming for post-Pesach.

Should I make a *folk dance movie* (and *guitar movie*), and do clips? What a novel idea, project, and good way to learn Adobe Premier Pro.

Possible Folk Dance Movie Titles and Ideas

Should it include folk dance tour clips? Why not?

And old and new video clips? Why not?

Mad Shoes, of course, is the perfect folk dance move. But would I want to make it? Would I want to, need to, change the script? (I don't want to simply repeat my old theme. . .or do I? Is there really anything else to add? I doubt it. Yet I want to go forward, not backward.

Maybe I'm talking about folk dance movies, but two *different* ones.

On the other hand, maybe I should produce a folk dance movie, and use all my social director organizational skills to get all my friends, contacts, business associates, and anyone else, together to make it.

Joy, power, strength, dancing fingers: the Mighty Mountain Volcano erupts, sending bright lava burning down the Tremolo

196 / JIM GOLD

River.

Preceded by the laugh piece: "Dancing Pavane in Peacock D."

I can break all the barriers only because I'm older. Older people have more choice. Or perhaps, they have *another* choice, because by now they're just too experienced and can't be fooled by phantoms knocking at the door or the same old nightmares breaking down their house. All those years of experience rip through them, stripping the old skin and pulling out the poisons of dried-up old habits and long-held thought patterns.

Saturday, April 20, 2024
Entering the Centered Land

The *Covid Wisdom Trilogy*. This to call the series after I publish my last Covid dancing book. Entering the centered land. I'm giving up advertising on Facebook. Pursuing, searching for new customers there is over; I'm giving up customer expansion. Finally, business-wise, I am centered. What a relief! Let them come to me.

I feel tremors, the first chills of happiness.

Could a limp be a symbol of fresh togetherness, centered focus, spiritual concentration similar to what happened to Jacob (James) after he wrestled with God? (Being a heel works!) Although leaving the match with a limp, he ended up centered, focused, and became the leader. Can one have a happy limp, deliciously painful knees? (Union in conflict, united in struggle?) I do feel very good about the whole thing.

Living in the Moment

It's about *how* to live in the moment, having the courage to. What is the mystery beneath the notes, beneath the dance steps, behind the images of the world?

Sunday, April 21, 2024

Play like a child in the Garden of Eden. Is that what's it's really all about? There's nothing you can hold on to. Except God. But God is so fluid. Can you learn to feel good about holding on the fluid? Is that what playing in the Garden of Eden is all about?

Monday, April 22, 2024
Back to Depression but with A Fresh Twist

Yesterday, I noticed a deliciousness in my downs. I "enjoyed" the feelings, even relished them.

Are depressions creative? Yes.

They're all about return, but with a fresh twist.

Finding new ways to complain about body parts, the political and world situations, and many other things (this taboo subject is no longer taboo).

Strange parts of my old self have returned, pieces I hated and always wanted to avoid. But after five years of trying to handle and eliminate them, even succeeding for a few months (or was it weeks?), yesterday's chill made me realize I miss them.

I know why. Depression forces me to be creative. (Note "forces," not "chooses." A breath of life.)

So I'm returning to depression with a fresh appreciation and understanding of its power. In fact, I'd call it a secret power. (And one that should not be "cured.")

Sinking and rising are the rhythm of life.

I appreciate any wave that comes along. Evidently, going, and being, down generate a life force that lifts me up.

With a refund on depression entering my coffers, what dividends will it bring?

Complaints are creative. (As long as they're "interesting.") For me, they're often expressed indirectly through fiction. Perhaps this will force me to write fiction to escape from the pit.

At this stage of life, the main subject is death and what we are going to do about it.

Maybe there is no maybe.

Tuesday, April 23, 2024
"Dive In and "Just Do It" Ride Again

I sense a whiff of optimism and hope this morning. Discouragement and downs have temporarily fled. To my amazement, I feel *rested and better.* Could "mere" rest have done it? Maybe. The Soviets believed in the rest cure. Or is it accepting the *possibility* of knee surgery? Truth is, I may never know why. And it really doesn't matter. I crossed the line. Today I feel great, full of optimism and hope! Can I believe in this, especially after yesterday felt so bad? Always the conflict between transience and seizing the moment, otherwise called loving what I've got. I'm afraid the good feelings will disappear. And they will! The skill is learning to dive into the now and milk their essence.

Big transitional idea today: Seeing tours as my toys, my playthings; HubSpot and Stripe, too. (Adding book sales, videos, guitar, and folk dancing are afterthoughts, and as such, hopefully may come later.) Also an old idea revisited: Next career as a writer: Two hours every morning. The Babble Bible: Opening strokes.

Wednesday, April 24, 2024
(How to) Use My Fear to Improve My Life

Pleasant or unpleasant, friend or foe, *fear* will never go away. The question is: *How to use it?*

One good approach is to turn its energy outward on the world, to help change it by doing a better job, always improving what you do (which means what you give). It's the *tikkun olam* approach.

In other words, turning my fear on myself, and (instead of having it paralyze me) using its energy to improve and move forward.

Fear resides in my abdomen, and so does my power.

Energy is the big thing. Fear is only one of its venues (but a big one).

Five-Day Slip into the Old Neighborhood

Touched off by five successful repetitions of my new squat exercise, coupled with an increase of left-leg lymphedema swelling—touched off in turn by two months of the sitting to study and learn modernizing computer programs, plus the usual "standard" knee pains, all combined to create a wave of adrenaline-shot fear. Its blast blew me back.

But this morning, rationally, reasonably, I realized nothing has changed. I am in the same good place as before this five-day battering.

The storm has ended; clouds have lifted. I can move on.

Now I understand what happened: An old self put-down mechanism returned. My excitement, really exhilaration, over the success of the five-squat exercise was shut down when I created a storm of Doom thinking. I slipped, easily aided by some lymphedemic swelling and a bit of knee pain, familiar ways of dealing with success.

But it's post-Covid time. Excitement and exhilaration are on the rise with their own interpretations of reality.

Thursday, April 25, 2024
The Tiger's Mouth

An unusual period: strange feelings of stiffness, heaviness, resistance, all because I succeeded.

Success has closed all my exit roads and opened the future. A door is wide open. To what? I *must* perform.

Performing will take the form of "only" making videos. But it is still performing.

Standing before the tiger's mouth, I face destruction and creation. Performing is my last road. If I don't take it, I shrivel up and die. If I do, I create again and live!

And turn fear into excitement!

Performing is *not* my tour business. Tours are my social, social-directing, fun, money-making sideline.

With a return to (some kind of) performance, the Covid Trilogy has served its purpose, run its course, and ended.

CHAPTER EIGHT

Postscript

Friday, April 26, 2024
Knees Revisited: The Drafty, Slow, Torturous
Decision-Making Process

Should I even enter my decision process into this journal? Who'd be interested? On the other hand, does it matter? After all, I write this journal to discover myself. It has nothing to do with others.

The big question is: Should I get a knee-replacement operation? (I'd start with the left knee.) Other questions emerge: Will it help my lower back, improve morning stiffness, aches, and pains? Is a strong exercise-and-stretching program better? Or should they work side by side? Questions fog and flood my mind: Will such an operation distract me from the emptiness of success, dispel the void? What about stairs? The Religion of Movement is my cure and salvation. But does it need help? Will my knees only get worse—even if I exercise? Will they stabilize, with exercise?

Can they improve, get better through my religion of exercise? I believe maybe they can.

Folk Dancing Videos

Here is a purpose: Aim my videos at my Monday and Wednesday class folk dance students, then aim them at students throughout the world! To learn my dances. Make them teaching videos. And right out of my living room "studio," too.

Saturday, April 27, 2024

Correct guitar playing means the *tikkun olam* guitar-playing method. The proper focus is: Every note I play and project heal myself and the world. Which comes first, myself or the world? Put the world first, then myself (even though the "natural" way is the opposite. But by doing so, by distracting myself from myself, I heal myself faster. And when I heal faster, the world heals faster.

I've been battered and scattered lately, distracted from my path. I need to find some anger energy, perhaps in the form of self-disgust, that will push me upward, funnel my scattered efforts into a focus. Stop wasting my time on trivia and noise. I have important things to do, namely, healing myself and the world.

How do I do that?

Focus my energy on the art, business, and sales tasks I must perform. Videos (guitar and folk dance), writing (bio), exercise, selling tours (business and sales connect me to the world), and language study as a brain warm-up.

Aches, worries about body parts, although they must be dealt with on some level, are still just fancy distractions from the prime task.

How did I get so thrown? Transition clouds perhaps. But clarity is coming.

Heal thyself and the world with it. Use the talent and skills given me. That is my task and contribution. Everything else is noise and distraction.

Joy, Fun, Play the Pavane

No question joy cures. In order to bring joy to others, I have to bring it to myself. Can I give it in the "Pavane in A" fast scale passage? Play, relish it? My challenge. Try it. Do it.

Bringing joy to the world is pretty good. Not much to do beyond that. (But I have to be the *example*. If I can't do it for myself, I can't do it for others.)

Reaching for joy is a difficult but worthy task. The body (folk dance, exercise), and fingers (guitar) have to be warmed up before they can feel and express joy. Since joy is the cure: If I write the *Jim Gold Life*, my first task (radically new) is to make it fun, enjoy it.

Now there's my post-Covid challenge and radically new path. The task, challenge, life rule is: I have to enjoy it, love, relish, dive in, luxuriate in it.

How to practice joy? Imagine its flow in my legs, fingers, muscles, and more. How about adding knees, and lower back, too?

Power is not joy. But the doorway to joy is power. Playing guitar, I feel the power in the tips of my "Alhambra" tremolo fingers. And that is good. But it is not joyful. Although it feels strong and healthy, it's still a warm-up. But it's getting close.

Sunday, April 28, 2024
Adventures with Joy Energy—Wrestling with Joy

I had eight hours of sleep last night. This morning I feel rested, clearer, stronger, more optimistic. Evidently, the Soviet sleep cure works, at least to a degree.

Rest cleans, clears, lightens, and lights up the mind.

It takes lots of energy and power to stay up and focused. I'm drained and tired. I need a joy break. Doing mundane things is my rest-and-relax vacation from the heights.

Monday, April 29, 2024

I'm in shock; I'm truly considering having a knee replacement operation. But after floating in Super Stunned land for the past few days, I'm steadying, and preparing for the challenge. How?

First comes the research phase: Call and talk to everyone I know. Second (or maybe first): Continue positive routines and rituals. Also, can one *train for this operation?* If yes, how?

Guitar: *Warm-Up Has Its Own Truth*

Not a good idea to "use" pieces ("Pavane in C") to warm up with. Better are traditional legato, scales, and arpeggio. Then dive into the pieces, with full joy energy.

Warm-up (as warm-up) has its own truth.

Use it for its own good-in-itself purpose.

Then move on to pieces.

On Understanding the Essence of Tremolo: *Truth of the Tremolo*

Idea: Practice arpeggio warm-up strong (and loud) to feel and prepare for the final step: Joy energy in every piece I play. Yes, I can and should go right into tremolo after my strong arpeggio warm-ups! ("Alhambra" or any other.)

After warm-ups, dive into joy energy right away. Accept and deepen the truth of the tremolo—which is the bass. The tremolo (a, m, i classical, or i, a, m, i flamenco) is the tickle on top of the essence. It's important, but it is still a tickle. The essence, expressed through thumb (p) remains fundamental, prime, bottom, and foundation.

Does music have a truth? Is it a vibration I can live by, in, and with?

What does all this mean as far as lifestyle and philosophy is concerned? Remember the important things (what's important, the fundamentals), but enjoy the tickles (passing clouds, transient events).

Tuesday, April 30, 2024

My job is put the ship in the water, be patient, and let it sail.

Wednesday, May 1, 2024
Knees and More

After my long walk and gym yesterday, my knee worries are fading. Can I trust my mind? Was mine a slip into the past in new form?

Guitar Freedom Manifest

Is this what my post-Covid transformation is all about? And do I really need two to three weeks of physical knee, leg, and lower back-stiffness misery to solidify the transformation in mind and body?

It manifested this morning while playing the Sor "Etude Number 12."

I've added a significant "I don't care anymore" to my playing, which has loosened me up (totally). I dare to play faster, lighter, easier, and a bit sloppier. But allowing this is freeing me.

Also, in "Alhambra," I'm replacing the tremolo nostalgia with: "Marvel and enjoy the clarity of thumb!" (And note the shadow fingers get better *too* in the process.)

Thursday, May 2, 2024
Connections

I like connections. Is there a connection between my thumb and knee? Is there a connection between "Alhambra," the importance of bass, and thumb as an instrument of deep, fundamental expression, and the knee with its functions of running, walking, dancing, and standing in place?

There are no endings, only new levels, next stages.

What about the physical symbols? Teeth, knees, attitude, layers, levels?

Note the Hebrew word for knees: *barak*. Its other meanings, beyond "blessing," are "power," "growth," and "spur prosperity."

What is the *barak* blessing of a new knee?

Post-Covid transformations, now in physical form, continue.

Friday, May 3, 2024

I'm somewhat sad, melancholic over the loss of self-definition as artist. But also partially relieved. The pressure is off.

Art can be used in the service of business. Making money means serving people. Greed is really the strong desire to serve, please, belong to, and be part of *others*. Money symbolizes service in green form. That's why I love it so. I love to serve, be useful, wanted, and needed.

The artistic burden, and its crust of slavery, are being stripped away. Blown up, broken apart, scattered in all directions, uncertain, and melancholic.

Art as business laboratory.

Reborn as a businessman. What does that mean? Take mathematics seriously.

Everything that used to mean so much doesn't mean so much anymore. For example, two styles of "Alhambra"—fast and slow. Two totally different modes. And that's okay, because it no longer much matters how I play them. After all, who cares about how a businessman plays guitar? Totally beside the point. The whole concept of a businessman playing guitar, especially classical guitar, is so strange, different, absurd, and ridiculous.

What freedom this new self-definition gives me! As the old world fades into melancholy oblivion, I realize the blessing.

I used to think business and making money were a grand annoyance. I had to fulfill my business obligations and responsibilities before I could be free to do what I really want to do: create art, be an artist.

But now things have been reversed. The obligation and annoyance factor are gone. I'm free to do art with no artistic obligations or responsibilities to fulfill, no fast or slow, no expression or no expression, nothing. It's *rubato* freedom all the way. I just played the freest "Gavotte in D" ever.

And business may turn out to be lots of fun. My public arena playpen. Imagine that!

Saturday, May 4, 2024
Enthusiasm Break

I'm taking an enthusiasm break. What does that feel like? Give in to the feeling of destruction of everything I once thought, follow it down the cleansing path to the end, where creation lies. Then let re-creation take its revitalizing course.

Eliminating fears blocking excitement, giving them up, is an exhausting process. But it has happened. So basically, after what feels like a five-year "Covid" break, rest, vacation, it's about returning to the "fun" things I did, but with mind cleaner, clearer, and filled with rekindled enthusiasm.

Truth in Guitar: The Life of Fingers

What's guitar playing all about? Guitar truth is world truth. When all the fingers are united in one hand, fear will be eliminated, and unity, peace, and love will prevail.

Although they'll never be equal in size and strength, all fingers must be equal in opportunity—to create and take their proper place.

Here's a truth: Fear created the knot; excitement loosened, untied it. Sor "Etude Number 12" is flying. (Released and free to fly.)

Guitar: Aim to play for the pleasure and curiosity.

I know it works.

Tuesday, May 7, 2024
It's All Up to Me

I've cleaned up my act, and I'm ready to roll, which means I'm ready to perform again.

But I have no audience to perform *for*. Oh, yes, I can make videos of my guitar playing or folk dancing. But that is not a *real* audience, with real flesh and blood, one that is seen, heard, smelled, and felt in front of me.

Truth is I *have* no real audience to perform for. Nor am I looking for one.

Although I like work, I have no need to do it. To perform in public again is not necessary, at least for the old reasons.

The finale of this adventure came two weeks ago. I completed my Adobe Premiere video and HubSpot learning project. Plus, I realized that, after a nine-month trial period, advertising on Facebook did not work. All the money and time I put in to hiring a digital marketer to expand my folk tour business had failed.

So in a friendly firing, I dropped him. I also dropped the idea, shall I say the dream, of expanding my tour business.

Ah, that's the key word: *dream*. Although I hesitate to admit it, expanding my tour business beyond its small folk dance audience has always been my dream. During my entire career, I've never succeeded in doing this, but I always had the hope, the *dream*, that I could.

When I fired my digital marketer, I gave up my dream. Losing it was also accompanied by learning HubSpot—to improve my emails—and Adobe Premier—to improve my choreography and folk dance group videos. I had hoped all of these would expand my tour business.

So, lots of *dreams of tour expansion died* when these projects were completed. But happily, the final realization was: *I'm doing just fine on my own.* Sure, its "nice" to have beautifully designed emails and professional-looking videos. But business-wise, customer-wise, it makes no difference. Creating pretty stuff gives me lots of personal satisfaction, and personal motivation is *very important.* But beyond that, for business, sales, and marketing, it has little purpose.

Where am I now?

I fell into a Sarnoian TMS funk, a familiar retreat with its usual distracting, self-created aches and pains whose culmination was the idea of having knee replacement.

But will knee replacement cure ontological pains? Will it replace lost dreams and instill new purpose? I doubt it. (It might be good for other reasons, and I may still need it someday, or even now. I'll see what Dr. Klein says after my examination this Thursday.)

Meanwhile, the emptiness from losing tour expansion dreams has been replaced by the gut-felt knowledge that growth and expansion, if it ever comes, are all up to me. And truth is: They have always been all up to me!

Strangely, the loss of these dreams, along with the certainty that *it's all up to me*, give me more strength and confidence.

Wednesday, May 8, 2024
True and New Purpose of Guitar

Play guitar, not to perform or improve, but to *cure*, to heal, and in this process, to enliven and elevate.

Thursday, May 9, 2024
The Non-Performing Life

Frustration is part of learning. I need to learn to love it.

When I look back on my life, the first vision I had—at the end of high school—was "Einstein-in-the-attic." I was sitting at a bridge table in the attic with a floor lamp beside me. The table was strewn with books, mostly on physics and philosophy. My goal was to study the secrets of the universe.

What a beautiful vision! It was mirrored by all-day weekend violin practice, followed by late-afternoon basketball played with fellow humans sometimes called my friends, but not always.

Later, when I got married, I chose performing on guitar as my profession. I *had* to perform, because I had to make a *living*. That was the rule of marriage.

Guitar and performing thus became irreparably linked. In this way, I always felt somewhat "forced" into the performing life. Like an albatross around my neck, the obligation to do so, weighted with heavy financial responsibilities, never left me.

How could I ever dislodge myself from its powerful grip? Such freedom was almost unthinkable.

I'd need a cosmic explosion to free myself. Well, along came a crippling knee experience, strong enough to shatter the old image and free my mind from the habitual weight of the performing life.

Two weeks ago, I concluded my post-Covid cleansing search. Pure and fresh, I was ready to step back into the performing world without brakes, ready to restart.

But to my paralyzed amazement, I couldn't do it. My mind exploded in frustration and anger. Finally ready to roll, I couldn't. Instead, my knee fell apart, followed by other parts of my body. Stymied, I had to ask myself, "Is performing what I want? Was returning to the performing life the *real* reason I used the Covid break to clean up my act?

My conclusion: Maybe I don't want or need an albatross around my neck again. Maybe freedom from this monster is what I was really searching for all along. To take a new path was difficult and frightening, especially after treading the same road for so many years. How to break free from such a prison chain? Maybe only a crippling knee explosion could do it, a surgical procedure that would blast away the used-up thoughts and replace them with a new, pure baby one.

What was my original dream? A life of study and learning, dedicated to uncovering the secrets of the universe, of adventure spiced with curiosity and wonder. Add playing teenage basketball, or folk dancing, as an adult sport of choice for social life with fellow humans. Could the collapse of my knee be part of a long-term freeing and healing? I love the idea. It gives such cosmic purpose and meaning to all this frustration and pain.

Friday, May 10, 2024
Christian Science and Jewish Science in a Nutshell

The body is a by-product of the mind.
The mind is a by-product of the soul.

The soul is a by-product of the Spirit.
Think this way, and I'll be healed.

Went to Dr. Klein yesterday. He said, with the lymphedema
swelling in my left knee, healing from a knee replacement operation would be slow, not certain, and questionable, so he wouldn't
do it. I'd first have to bring the swelling down—a lot. Then he
gave me a list of three lymphedema doctors to see.

Finally, I got an excruciatingly painful knee cortisone shot.

Klein's diagnosis completely threw me. I never expected it.
Presently, doctors and most research say that lymphedema is in-
curable and can only be "managed." To me that means a knee replacement operation will *always* be "iffy," even dangerous, and
might even make things worse!

Even if I could succeed in bringing down the swelling, manage
it, the operation would still remain in the "iffy" category. Who
wants "iffy," especially from an operation? I walked out whipsawed, confused, stunned, and buffeted. Even so, I set up a date
for surgery in late August,

After we came home, I began to feel the effects of the cortisone
shot. Amazing: Left knee pain was 90-95 percent gone! It made
me think that, if I can swing it, an operation would be a yes.

So now, the next big step is to research lymphedema, see the
new doctors Klein recommended. Also, I wonder about alternative
medicine and its approaches. Has anyone ever *healed* lymphedema?

Moving on another cosmic level, the metaphysical, mystical,
astrological, and kabbalistic questioning one: Slowly, upon leaving the doctor's office, I began to feel totally relieved and happy.
I didn't *have to* have an operation. I'll wait, postpone, and think.
For now I'll return to the wonderful life I was leading a mere two

weeks ago.

I also wonder if Dr. Klein's "no" saved me from an operation in order to see if there's another way to manage myself, or better.

Post-Cortisone Life

I needed to put our laundry in the basement washing machine. So I walked down the stairs. How "pleasant" and good my left leg thigh and knee now felt. Even the stiffness felt pleasant.

Dwell on the pleasant.

Don't jump ahead to the end.

Can pain and pleasure be integrated into the Chill of Magnificence?

Saturday, May 11, 2024
Play

Last night, I opened HubSpot and tried to figure out how to create new email layouts. I asked Google for a tutorial. No luck. I looked up the HubSpot Knowledge Center. Also nothing.

Then I said to myself: I'll just "play" with the HubSpot site, and see what happens. I did. . .and I figured it out!

Then I copied my new Adobe Illustrator program from my main computer to my laptop. I opened it, quickly glanced through a couple of tutorials, then decided to bypass them and try "playing" with the AI program. Slowly, I also began figuring *that* out. Amazing and fun.

Thinking about play, I went to sleep. I had a dream: I was warming up for folk dance teaching by dancing "Tsadik Katamar." A small group of folks sitting in the corner cheered when I finished. I've never had a dream where folks cheered me merely for an "alone" practice session. (What could it mean?)

I woke up after a wonderful seven-hour sleep, still in shock about how good my left knee felt! I had coffee, began Hebrew study, and tried to do it in last night's Adobe Illustrator play mode. (It partly worked.) Maybe my new cortisoned knee is a symbol of a fresh future, light and free.

But before I could, I had two more weeks of transition hell, with its whipsaw modes, increased lymphedema, crippling left knee pains, ending with contemplations of knee replacement.

It felt like the finale of a grand transition.

But the true finale had been my visit to Dr. Klein. His unexpected decision not to do knee replacement surgery due to my lymphedema had totally unnerved me. But it also freed my mind. Walking out of his office, I slowly began to feel better and better; this soon transformed into feeling great!

Maybe my old knee, with its aches, pains, and lymphedema, is a symbol for my antiquated lifestyle whose negative attitudes were wiped away during my four-year Covid transition. That's finished. It disappeared two weeks ago, when I knew I was ready to move on.

I'm almost ready for my next *New Leaf Journal*. I think it's title will be *Play*. I have a free weekend to contemplate and absorb all this. Can this "play attitude" be applied to lymphedema? Could it be my personal discovery, my miracle cure? And also maintain the cortisoned miracle improvements in my knee? What a thought!

It is in my power to *choose it* as a positive direction, a wonderful road to travel—no matter where it leads.

Note, as an aside, and perhaps another symbol: I look outside: What a beautiful day! Clear blue sky, sun shining, temperature cool and perfect, easy, light, and free.

A time to relish, remember, and use this pain-free, clear sky, humble life, and ride with them.

My left knee goes with lymphmedemic swelling, and a new heart. All are metaphors and symbols. With God's help, could I turn them into material reality?

I know, on one level, my choice is His choice, and vice versa. He supports *our* effort.

A New Life

A new business: Jim Gold international Travel Agency or JGI Travel (Cathie was the angel on this one), a new knee (Dr. Klein was the angel on this one), a new way of walking (I was the angel on this one), a renewed way of stretching (Jorge from Bolivia at the gym was the angel on this one), and a revival of the old great "miracle schedule" routines and rituals, but this time even better (I was the angel on this one). A new life!

Artist and Agent: Art (Creation) and Business

"Agent" is a powerful word. Agents make things happen. Art is a skill. Act is a movement. An artist must act just as an actor must create art.

So what?

I'm trying to connect artist to agent, and vice versa, and ultimate, art to business and vice versa. And this because I am both. And as a travel agent, I will be both.

CHAPTER NINE

Light Touch

Monday, May 13, 2024
Light Touch and the Ad-Man's Life

I'm fresh, new, rested, and weary of ancient, heavy ways.
Dispel what's heavy.
Ride into Land of the Light Touch.

Co-Opt Failure as Part of the Light

Again the Specter of Failure returns.
But she is an old friend now.
Perhaps even she can be co-opted into the light.

Light guitar is not something you can *practice*.
It has to rise organically from the Light.

Ladder of Light

The lighter you go, the faster you go, until you reach the speed of light.
Is the speed of light a good place to be?
Well, it's not bad. . . . Or maybe its neutral, beyond good and bad.
But in this world, the ladder of light is a good one to climb.

Tuesday, May 14, 2024
Lessons of Wounded Knee

Suddenly, after a morning of good stretching and several days of great gym stuff, my left knee collapsed. I could hardly walk, much less teach my Monday night dance class. Shocking. I'd lost the peace, calm, quiet, and security of my cortisone shot. How strange? Why now? I wondered.

But there was a folk dance gain: Due to the injury, I had to let my dance students take over the class. They were "forced" to lead. Soon the benefits of my injury became obvious as they slowly succeeded. I put on dances most everyone knew. And they all ended up have a great time! A wonderful evening was had by all.

Generals need lieutenants and captains in the fight for folk dance happiness. I run the class, lead, but on a different level. I hate learning this lesson, but it is useful and a wonderful growth form.

So when my left knee starts speaking to me (in its annoying way), I need to focus on this "pass it on to others" lesson.

Using the new techniques I'm learning in HubSpot emails, Adobe Premiere Pro videos, and even Adobe Illustrated (some day) fliers, ads, and posters, is the first step.

That is their dynamic, wild-and-fresh purpose.

Wednesday, May 15, 2024

Can a light touch be practiced without warm-up? Or as a mental practice, is it its *own* warm-up? Does one start with the *thought* of a light touch—then put it into practice? The answer is yes: A Light Touch thought starts immediately. It *precedes* both "warm-up" or diving into the piece itself. Thought precedes action. Thinking "light touch" *is* the practice.

Can I tighten my abs with a light touch? Yes.

In fact, tightening abs while playing guitar helps you relax the fingers!

Travel at Its Best!

A light touch also signals a sense of humor. I wonder if I have any sense of humor left? And if I do, what form, if any, will it take post-Covid? Fantasy fiction, more off-the-wall tales? Can I add a sense of humor to guitar, folk dancing, even business? It sure would give things a light touch and make them much more fun.

Humor and Light Touch

I'd love to resurrect humor and inject it into everything I do: bring my crazy into the real world. What a flight that would be!

Can it be *practiced?* I'm not sure. Humor is truly a gift of and from God, grace descending in transparent, diaphanous, wiggly angel form.

My Muse of A-Muse-ment, so suppressed, and for so long: I cry, break down in tears because I want her so.

Maybe this signals her first appearance.

She is so missed!

Maybe humor confers the light touch, and vice versa.

But you can't force her. She has to rise organically out of the ashes.

Thursday, May 16, 2024

Empty and aching again. Watch out for yesterday's highs. Whipsaw continues but is lessening. Plus yesterday, in the late afternoon, I added light touch guitar practice.

Note: my lymphedema is down to almost nothing. I wonder why. The positives are slowly falling into place. Stay calm and steady.

Light Touch Starts Immediately

Start Light Touch practice right away, since no muscles will be strained. (But the abs kick in immediately.)

Friday, May 17, 2024
Blink and Blank Path to Satisfaction and Happiness

Is satisfaction happiness? Or maybe simply a step below ecstasy? But no question that satisfaction and happiness come with technical mastery. Thus focus on technical mastery is a path to them. Thus the beauty and importance of learning something deeply and well.

Creating Focus Flow Uproot Mental Clinging

When discovery of a truth burns through the brain, should one dwell on its magnificence, wonder, and beauty? Let it "sink in," force it to say in place, hold on, and keep it? Or destroy its transient dwelling place of security and false permanence?

Social Director of the Folk Dance Group

I've solved the dance problem. I don't *have to* dance.

I can dance—or not. Either way is good. (And sometimes, when I don't, it's even better for the group!)

I'm really *social director* of the folk dance group.

Saturday, May 18, 2024
Battle of Wounded Knee Revisited

Since Dr. Klein's cortisone shot, not only has pain in my knee disappeared, but I've noticed a mild instability appearing in the kneecap. But none on the inside (as it used to be).

Is this a sign of TMS? I like this idea. But am I right?

After months of being the heroic owner of knee pain, after one mere shot of cortisone, it is gone! Wonderful! But also strange, different, and, perhaps, even threatening.

Regarding My Wife

In youth physical beauty;
in older age, a different kind of beauty emerges
with the addition of elegance and wisdom.

The "Knee Too" Movement

My "Knee Too" movement signifies the end of self-sabotage.

Sunday, May 19, 2024
Dwell in the Dissonance

Crossing into a summer period of calm and creative focus, with nothing exciting on the horizon—and that's okay.

All notes even: a calm tremolo summer, vast and empty, not sad or depressing, nor happy or elevating, but calm, quiet, different, and interesting, wide open and narrow, plus vice versa.

This couldn't be good. But it doesn't feel bad, either.

No pressure to achieve, reach, attain, expand, or grow, but lots of tools in stock for a welcoming spell of summer exploration and self-entertainment, to run wild across an open field of fascination. This is beginning to sound exciting!

Monday, May 20, 2024
A "Just Do It" Day

Yesterday at the early family birthday-cum-Memorial Day party, a victory. Without noticing it, a giant leap. I picked up the guitar, before others, and without thinking, focused on the pleasure of playing; I didn't even notice the audience. (A distant haze in my mind of *don't annoy me, I want to focus.*)

True victory comes when you don't even want, need, or remember to even mention it. You just do it.

Don't write about it in my published journal. Hand-written directions, personal, for-the-day, slowly absorbed, and once absorbed, ultimately forgotten, are okay.

Tuesday, May 21, 2024
Let the Music Roll!

Do less and dive deeper. Continue marching along down to the syllable in Hebrew and French songs.

Hope and discouragement form and pass, come and go, expand, diminish, then join the flow. Begin my light touch practice.

Start with guitar: Focus on hot blood flowing. Do it right away as right-hand fingers, thumb, index, middle, ring, touch the 5,3,2, 1 strings of C chord, and left hand grip of the four opening notes of Milan's "Pavane in C."

Then, after playing awhile, put the guitar aside. Add folk dance exercises, arms, legs, neck, torso, all, as the body joins a dive into hot blood flow.

Integrating guitar and exercise. Mixed stretching. Discover the guitar notes in my body. Break through perfection practice walls. Cut holes in the ceiling, and let the trials and tribulations of life drip through: Violence and pain are part of life. Add them to my repertoire. How to use the breakthrough power of pain and violence to grow my guitar playing? The power of playing fast, very fast, is a good start. Throw caution to the wind.

Wednesday, May 22, 2024
Light Touch and the Ad-Man's Life

Adam was the first man. Ad-Man is close.

Adam and Eve as the first couple are similar to Ad-Man and

Eve. How does Eve fit in? She's eve-r my inspiration.

What's new?

Descent (through the knee) creates the energy of ascent. Here's how it works:

My "Knee Too" movement has created focus on my folk dance classes and groups dancing without me, or rather with me leading from the side, or behind, or whatever. But not necessarily out there. This is *good for the group.* And good for me too, in a knee too way. I can also promote my choreos by teaching, training the group to dance them correctly and better. This is also good for the group.

Birth of "Knee Too" Movement

I began this morning frozen in old knee terror, stiff with the usual fear and trepidation. But I chose to write about these emotions *only* by hand, not enter them into my computer-generated *New Leaf Journal.* Why? Because they are "old stuff." I've said these things countless times before; they are getting boring.

Can one be bored by terror, fear, and trepidation? Can they remain the same if they become boring? Are these powerful emotions losing their energy and ability to fool me, thereby giving up their reality? I hope so.

The Knee Too movement means giving up terror, fear, and trepidation, losing their reality, and letting my warrior and fighter self win out.

Thursday, May 23, 2024

Could pain, like ignorance, not belong to the real me? Passing clouds *look* real. And like all material things, in their transitory form, they are invested with the aura of reality.

Looking at the bigger picture though, thinking long-term,

they're worth a nod but not much else.

Can a mind create its own cortisone shot? In the process, fix my knee real fine?

Friday, May 24, 2024
Strong Guitar Sound Color

To my light touch add *strong*. Right-hand fingers placed near the bridge, the *third spot:* tough, metallic, strong sound. Even try it with fingers placed between bridge and sound hole—the *second spot,* or moderate spot (between tough and sweet). *First spot:* Sweet spot, fingers placed over sound hole.

Play a strong Milan "Pavane in A," even its "fast" scale.

Accents

Another way to play strong is through accents: adding, emphasizing them. Note the 3/4 time in Fernando Sor's "Etude Number 12." So playful and joyful with accent focus on the first beat.

The Pressure Is Off

All pressures on my guitar have been lifted, and now playing is nice and easy.

Same thing just happened with folk dancing. Having my group members lead the dances has freed me, taken the pressure off my feeling that I *have to dance* (no matter what). I wonder if it will affect, take the pressure off, the body parts where I feel it most—namely, my legs, ankles, and knees.

I wonder if, as pressures diminish, will knee pain, and even arthritis diminish with them? Will bone-on-bone turn into tone-on-tone? Of course, these are *wishes.* But I wonder if any material reality could come out of them.

Saturday, May 25, 2024
Flowing and Strong

I'm trading "differently," using larger and more stable companies. I *am* in a new place. Somehow I believe that now I will succeed.

My knee hurts this morning. Discouraging. But keep going. I used to think pain is a given. Also a fresh thought: Old—is pain a "given? Live and deal with it. Now I ask myself: Is it a *reminder of my self-healing goals?*

Also note the importance of a mental attitude: As my mind goes up and down, whipsawed between optimism, improvement, and hope, and pessimism, despair, and hopelessness, so goes my knee—up and down.

Also on the positive side: Last night's guitar playing: flowing and strong! (What is a self-healing knee but flowing and strong!)

As for this last volume of the Covid Trilogy: Since my next *New Leaf Journal* will be called *Wide Open,* why not end the Covid Trilogy in a *wide open* manner? Let it slowly drain away.

What Has Covid Taught Me?

What has Covid taught me? The path of the world is wide open. *Wide open!* There are no endings. Only diaphanous upward improvement cycles of beginning, ending, and new beginning.

Nothing lasts, but nothing dies.

Sunday, May 26, 2024
Zohar Guitar

Pavane C, A, and D: Maximum right hand plucking power (between rosette and bridge), but with limits (soft-pressing left hand). Zohar guitar means thinking and playing brilliantly but within limits. Note *Zohar* means "brilliant shining" but also "warning: not too extreme, remember limitations."

Play to wake the dead! The sleeping python rises.

"Pavanes," "Sor 12," and "Alhambra" are rolling. They now reside in the Zohar practice bag. So too Bach's "Gavotte in D" and "Gavotte in Rondeau."

On to "Leyenda" and the summer challenge: Crossing, breaking, passing through the "Leyenda" barre-passage wall.

A python power morning. Stop at my victory, glow a bit, and move on.

Let The Sweetness In

Late afternoon "Pavane": Power, competence, and let the sweetness in.

Monday, May 27, 2024
Power in Bold Disguise

Yesterday I put "knee pain and Christian Science" into a Google search. I found all kinds of CS followers healed! No surgery, pills, injections, nothing. Happy and healed! Not bad for just believing.

I reread *Science and Health* by Mary Baker Eddy. Seems like Christian Science is similar to a Kabbalah healing practicum.

On one level, I've been thinking this way for years. I'm returning to CS to re-inspire and reconfirm my beliefs but now, as an older person, on a deeper level.

Could pain be power in disguise?

My routines and rituals are my road to strength. Sometimes, along the road, a thunderbolt of pain can serve as a wake-up call, a knock at the door. "Hello, your power has arrived."

Pain may serve as a secret signal of disguised power.

How to put this bold idea into practice by playing guitar? Heal myself (and others) as I play.

Tuesday, May 28, 2024
Self-Defining

I'm redefining myself as a tortured soul. Oh, sure, I smile a lot, have happy times, bring others happiness through my art forms, to my family through gatherings folk dancing, travel, lots of happy, happy, happy.

But merely because I have happy moments, happy days, and I *like* to be happy, I can't claim I'm not a tortured soul. Truth is, I mostly switch back and forth. Evidently, I thrive between agony and ecstasy. Tortured souls especially need the Divine.

Arrogance and Humility

I wonder if arrogance is causing me to injure myself. Arrogance means I take all the credit for my energy, lack of it, power, earnings, wisdom, accomplishments, failures, everything.

Humility is when I see myself as an instrument through which God works His wonders. We work together, share the burden; I take responsibility, but He runs the show. I'm quite happy with that arrangement. But how to *remember* it? And when I don't, arrogance steps in to take its place.

Guitar Concert: How to Put the Divine into Practice?

First piece: The Glory of God Pavane in C.

Stately, magnificent, gorgeous, the Glory rolls through the universe. Audiences smile under its radiance. Everyone is included.

Second piece: Pavane in A. A depressing visit to hell.

Third piece: "Purgatory Pavane" in D. Foggy, halfway house "Pavane,"announcing the illusion of entering the material world. The D major key offers glimpses of happiness but peppered with question marks.

So ends the "Pavane "Trilogy.

Next piece: Fernando Sor's "Etude Number 12."
A light waltzing into reality.

"Alhambra": Long fingers of the law reaching out; not sure what that means yet).

Wednesday, May 29, 2024
More Adventures of Tortured Soul: Advantages of Crawling at the Bottom

Does a tortured mind create a tortured body, one moving from annoying aches to one wracked with pain?

Or does a tortured body create a tortured mind, one annoyed by doubts and wracked with depression, discouragement, and darkness?

Obviously, body and mind work together. But which one comes first?

According to Kabbalah and Christian Science, it is the mind. Most scientists of the secular variety think it is the body.

I lean toward the Kabbalah view.

I used to think that to smile, be happy, not a victim, is for winners, while feeling discouraged, depressed, down, and crawling in darkness is for losers.

But most folks are *halfway* people: winner and loser, up and down, smile and frown, agony and ecstasy, opposites blended in contradiction, mysteries lost in facts.

There is a plus side to darkness. Lots of creative juices in those stagnant, smelly pools. Crawling at the bottom sometimes has its advantages.

Thursday, May 30, 2024
Easy/Natural Land Growing Pains

How easy today's Hebrew reading feels. Even guitar, travel, and earnings.

Folks are registering easily and naturally. Plus, I've added my winning new Private Tour business. I've won easy and natural, because I know the field.

Mental and spiritual changes need a different body to hold them, to fit the altered mind set. Growing pains are part of the process.

Friday, May 31, 2024
Entrepreneurship

Belief is a solid column. All the signs point in the same direction. I just have to say, "Yes!"

To what?

Self-definition as an entrepreneur.

As we watched *Shark Tank* on TV last night, suddenly, it occurred to me, not only that artist and businessman are one, but that, because this is true, I see myself as an entrepreneur.

Such a self-definition will not only clear my brain, but also resolve a lifetime conflict between art and business.

Is this shift in perspective mere nuance? But a nuance can signal a gigantic if slow change. A five-percent shift in direction can, over time, put you hundreds of miles away.

234 / JIM GOLD

An artist alone remains in the closet; a business alone remains separated from art. Fusing them together, an entrepreneur creates the synergy of union. So my divided self is closing.

With it, I feel a weight of responsibility ascending, an Atlas climbing on my shoulders. Is the shackled, directed energy of entrepreneurship a step toward liberty? Frost called writing poetry "moving easy in harness."

All the signs are there. I just have to say "Yes!"

I tremble with anticipation.

Saturday, June 1, 2024
Rest and Absorption

Since I don't feel like doing anything, feel tired and drained most of the time, this may show I "simply" need a rest, a break, time off, even a lot of it. After the castle blows up, debris and mud need to settle. I need to as well. Maybe, with guitar and everything else, I've gone as far as I can go, at least for now. And now might last a long time. A rest—even lasting a whole summer— could be needed. Or maybe even something totally different.

But what? Maybe my body is telling me something my mind does not want to believe. If my body feels broken and my spirit tired, with my mind in give-up mode, it may well simply mean I need this break. Very hard for me. Maybe hardest of all. Stop all activity. Lie around, sleep, waddle, wander, rest, find a nice ditch, and just lie there.

Monday, June 3, 2024
Exhausting the Subject

I've written enough about music and guitar. Perhaps it's the same for Hebrew, knees, aches and pains. I've exhausted these subjects.

In each area, I know what to do. And I'm doing it! What else is there to say about them? Probably nothing.

Send warm currents of relaxation from abs.

Wednesday, June 5, 2024
The Whipsaw Cloud

I'm writing after my visit to Dr. Kline. She said, "It's not lymphedema, it's venous stasis." To me, a quiet shocker. This means a knee replacement operation may be possible after all. Or not. Whipsawed once again. Thrown off the path. Should I, shouldn't I? Actually I still don't know. But I'm getting closer.

Results so far:

Whipsawed: My directional heart has been cut out from under me. No juice or purpose. All washed away. What's going on?

Well, just another form of the old gloom-and-doom, depression and despair black cloud of distraction passing over me. Really nothing new here. Only the amorphous shell, the outer misty cloud form, has changed. So, what is the answer to this new cloud formation? Easy. Just let it pass. Stay on the road, the finely carved miracle path it know and follow so well.

Complete Abs and"Alhambra" success. Dissolve and drop the amazement cloud distraction. Play it over and over again until the clouds dissolves, disappears, floats away by itself. (This may take a few days, even more.) Letting the abs-and-fingers wildcat out of the bag. I wonder where, and how far, this can go.

The awesome possibilities are scary. I'm peering into infinity. Is this what real running wild on the lawn can lead can to? Abs are the center of fear. But of excitement, too. Accept it (the whipsaw abyss) and move a step further.

Dwell in the Glow for a while; enjoy its shine of accomplishment. But also watch it pass.

Should one mourn the passing? Probably.

If you do, it means you really got into it, attached yourself to the Glow. I'd say that's a healthy, good thing. But good things are sad when they end.

The intense fatigue at the end of a bout of Glow is also part of it. I'd dive into that as well. Evidently, intense fatigue and mourning go together. I wonder if they are related, even different phases of the same emotion.

Are fatigue and mourning different sides of the same coin? A natural phenomenon to give in to, and not resist.

Friday, June 7, 2024

I don't believe in the old sources of motivation anymore. I've worn them out. They're all beside the point now.

The only thing that works is: Just do it.

Saturday, June 8, 2024
Post-Script: Out of the Wilderness

This morning started walking out of the wilderness with a new knee and leg. All without an operation.

How did it happen?

I played guitar last night; all tempos became fair game. This released my playing, and this morning it's still released!

Personal development mirrors biblical development. It begins by stepping into the guitar wilderness.

Ab focus and guitar freedom merged into a river of wisdom. The river said: "Slow is good, fast is good, medium is good. Tempos are feelings. All are good, only different." A happy "Alhambra" emerged.

My guitar choice of malady for many years may have been STS, suppressed thumb syndrome,

Sunday, June 9, 2024
Practical Approaches to "Just Do It"

Hebrew: First read the whole article through in its entirety before looking up words I don't know. (Try guessing their meaning from the context.)

Guitar:
Extend abs to shoulders in the "D major Pavane."
"Alhambra" tremolo: Connect abs to hypothenar thumb muscle the deepest of focused relaxation.

Monday, June 10, 2024
Three-Month Summer Goals

Limitation makes it real. Think three-month summer goals. See what happens.

1. New summer trading job starts. Yes. I'll try again, and succeed! How strange, strong and different is this bold statement? I will succeed! How do I know I am right? I don't.

2. Hebrew rolls with a first-read understanding.

3. Guitar: Start with neck and body stretches, fifteen minutes of pre-guitar body warm-up. Combine exercise and guitar. Unite body and guitar. Make them one, along with Judaism (*Yehood* means one, *yehad* means "unite," and both equal "Jewish." All three united in a trinity of worshiped Oneness. Not a bad start.

"Pavane in D": Released but a bit sloppy, edgy.

"Alhambra": Reaching out with the thumb is a whole different world. And a good one!

It's a new but ancient and rediscovered technique, pre-Alexander Bellow, and pro-RolandoVades-Blaine. Probably the way I used to play "Alhambra" without problems before my lessons with perfectionist Bellow, who, by telling me my tremolo was uneven and I should improve it, make it even by practicing it slowly, destroyed my tremolo, and with it my confidence in both tremolo and guitar playing. Can I blame him? *Should* I blame him? Well, why not? In the long run, was such destruction good for me? Can't say. But it sure created lots of problems. Now, with my thumb extended, reaching out, it feels right and true; I've returned home, come home again. Playing this way I can have confidence in tremolo and "Alhambra." I had it once, I lost it (for forty-five years), and found it again. The circle completes. Tara the Stonecutter. Quite amazing, this whole journey!

It seems so obvious now. Thumb out: A "mere" technical adjustment. But it took so long to get there.

Could it really be so simple? Maybe.

Birth of Self-Confidence as Seen in the "Alhambra" Story

Thumb out (reaching) in general and always. Is this the real way *I* play guitar? Comfortable, right, and natural. And even though I blame it on Bellow, it is *I* who somehow decided to block myself for years.

Was there an inner wisdom, a higher purpose, for doing such a thing? I'd like to think so. Otherwise, those years would be a total waste. I don't believe in waste. Deep down, I must have sensed some hidden reason. So I invented a twisted path to fulfill an inner need, give meaning to my life, by aiming to fulfill a higher purpose.

Maybe I needed my rocky side roads and journeys, with all

their blows, ups, downs, life on the edge, fights for financial and self-survival, in order to build self-confidence. And I have succeeded in doing that. I know what I'm doing in just about everything I do. I have self-confidence. Perhaps that is the real achievement.

About the Author

Jim Gold brings color to his worlds as a folk dance teacher, choreographer, musician, writer, tour organizer, and president of his travel company, Jim Gold International Folk Dance Tours.

His welcoming personality and enthusiasm for life inspires his folk dance students and travelers alike. He's also a classical and folk guitarist. His one-man show has appeared on TV and in schools and universities across the USA.

He has also written eleven books, many of which chronicle his varied life.